Robert Dessaix is a writer of fiction, autobiography and the occasional essay. From 1985 to 1995, after teaching Russian language and literature for many years at the Australian National University and the University of New South Wales, he presented the weekly *Books and Writing* program on ABC Radio National. In more recent years he has also presented radio series on Australian public intellectuals and great travellers in history, as well as regular programs on language. His best-known books, all translated into several European languages, are his autobiography *A Mother's Disgrace*; the novels *Night Letters* and *Corfu*; a collection of essays and short stories *(and so forth)*; and the travel memoirs *Twilight of Love* and *Arabesques*. In 2012 he published the collection of originally spoken pieces *As I Was Saying*, in 2014 the meditation *What Days Are For* and, in 2017, a guide to work and play in the twenty-first century, *The Pleasures of Leisure*. A full-time writer since 1995, Robert Dessaix lives in Hobart, Tasmania.

Also by Robert Dessaix

Novels
Night Letters
Corfu

Non-fiction
A Mother's Digrace
(and so forth)
Twilight of Love
On Humbug
As I was saying
What Days Are For
The Pleasures of Leisure

ROBERT DESSAIX

ARABESQUES

A TALE OF DOUBLE LIVES

b
BRIO

b
BRIO

Published in Brio by Xoum in 2017

Xoum Publishing
PO Box Q324, QVB Post Office,
NSW 1230, Australia
www.briobooks.com.au
www.xoum.com.au

ISBN 978-1-925589-00-9 (print)
ISBN 978-1-925589-01-6 (digital)

All rights reserved. Without limiting the rights under copyright below, no part of this publication shall be reproduced, stored in or introduced into a retrieval system, or transmitted in any form or by any means (electronic, mechanical, photocopying, recording or otherwise), without the prior permission of both the copyright holder and the publisher.

The moral right of the author has been asserted.

First published by Pan Macmillan Australia in 2008

Text copyright © Robert Dessaix 2008
Cover and internal design and typesetting copyright © Xoum Publishing 2017

Cataloguing-in-publication data is available from the National Library of Australia

Author photograph by Shane Reid
Cover design by Xou Creative, www.xoucreative.com.au
Printed and bound in Australia by McPherson's Printing Group

Papers used by Xoum Publishing are natural, recyclable products made from wood grown in sustainable forests. The manufacturing processes conform to the environmental regulations of the country of origin.

CONTENTS

Introduction	1
1. Algiers	6
2. Blidah	42
3. Tornac	60
4. Anduze	87
5. Morocco	109
6. Cuverville	128
7. Sousse	172
8. Biskra	196
9. So Be It	221

*We always write in order to remember the truth.
When we invent, it is only in order to remember
the truth more exactly.*

Luis Fernando Verissimo in
Borges and the Eternal Orangutans

*Home is heaven and orgies are vile,
But you need an orgy, once in a while.*

Ogden Nash

INTRODUCTION

'My whole life,' Jean-Jacques Rousseau once scribbled on the back of a playing card, 'has been nothing but a long reverie divided into chapters by my daily walks.' Although patently untrue—for a start he found time to father five children by his mistress and deposit them in a foundling home—it's a sentence that caught my attention when I first read it many years ago. It succinctly captured, I thought then, something fundamental about the shape of my own life (about which it was also plainly untrue).

It was the word 'reverie' that I was moved to ponder. In English it brings to mind nebulous daydreaming. Rousseau's *rêveries*, on the other hand, were anything but nebulous. In his *Rêveries du promeneur solitaire* (*Reveries of the Solitary Walker*), although he does maunder a bit, giving in from time to time to little bouts of self-pity and self-righteousness, he mostly bounces around in a continual flux of lively storytelling, reminiscences and meditation. Between lethal jabs at his many enemies, he ruminates on an extraordinary range of subjects, from happiness and the will of God to lying, novel-writing, growing chervil, Plutarch, King Gyges of Lydia, an old love from his youth and the nature of goodness. I still have my 1961 edition of this book with its faded blue cover. Looking at it now, I remember that on the whole I liked it very much.

Neither Plutarch nor King Gyges of Lydia makes an appearance in *Arabesques*—most of the other subjects I've mentioned do—but I undoubtedly owe Rousseau a debt of gratitude for awakening me as a writer to the possibilities of the reverie. In this book my 'walks' take me further afield than Rousseau's took him: the first one I write about is through the casbah in Algiers and my last on the seafront in Naples, and along the way I find myself in Portugal, Morocco, Normandy and the south of France. Yet the true vagabond in these pages is my mind. Very distantly, it is probably Jean-Jacques Rousseau who first let my mind off its leash to speak in the way it does.

He was a solitary walker, however. In only one of my chapters, the most obviously Rousseauesque, set in Biskra, Algeria, am I quite alone. I don't have the Frenchman's yearning for solitude. Everywhere I go, from the Sahara to the English Channel, I am companioned. To find a resting place in which to be alone with one's thoughts (in a pew in the Cathedral in Oporto, for instance, or the roof garden of a Neapolitan hotel) can be refreshing, but I generally seek out conversation. That is what enlivens my travels and, I hope, these reveries.

More importantly, though, on my first walk I bump into a man who isn't there. It's the writer André Gide, whose autobiography *If It Die* I first read as an adolescent while working in a Sydney bookshop. Gide then shadows me throughout the book, giving shape to my own thoughts on religion, love, ageing and why we travel (he was passionate about the same places I keep going back to). My encounters with Gide are a prism, as all our best conversations with friends are, ordering my thoughts on subjects of vital importance to both of us.

There is no account of Gide's life in *Arabesques*— that's not what this kind of encounter is about and there are, in any case, many biographies of this once famous French writer and intellectual. Unsurpassed amongst them is Alan Sheridan's *André Gide: a Life in the Present*. Gide's *Journals*, a literary triumph in their own right, also provide a detailed record of his life from 1889 almost until his death in 1951. However, in the English-speaking world where this man who was once the incarnation of French thought and letters is half-forgotten, he may need a brief introduction.

The bare bones of his life (and in this he reminds me of Rousseau) scarcely hint at its inner richness. For that you have to read his *Journals*, early works such as

Fruits of the Earth (1897), *The Immoralist* (1902) or *Strait is the Gate* (1909), or later works: for example, *The Vatican Cellars* (1914), *La Symphonie pastorale* (1919), *The Counterfeiters* (1926) and *If It Die* (also 1926). Even then, it's difficult sometimes to glimpse the passion and depth of thought beneath the brilliance of the style. As he said himself, although writing should be a kind of 'artesian gushing-forth', it should be regulated by reason, a critical spirit and the demands of art. In 1947 he was awarded the Nobel Prize for Literature and in 1952, just over a year after his death, the Suprema Congregatio Sancti Officii at the Vatican added his entire works, every last word of them, to its Index of Prohibited Books. I can see why: they are rife with both a Protestant spirit shading into out-and-out atheism and a scandalously unconventional sexuality.

From the moment he was born in Paris at the end of 1869 he seems to have lived at the cusp of two arcs. Or at least he liked to think so. His mother's family came from Normandy, while his father's had been settled for centuries in the Huguenot south; he was a Protestant in an overwhelmingly Catholic country; he was homosexual but married for forty-three years; he was a wealthy member of the haute bourgeoisie, yet in the company of Stalin on Red Square declared the Soviet Union to be the hope of mankind. Sweepingly, exhaustively cultivated, he spent half his life seeking to divest himself, layer by layer, of his own cultural wealth; in the chapel of his innermost self he hankered for the sensual tumult of the crossroads, while at the crossroads he feared the loss of his innermost self. In a word, he is hard to seize upon. Just when you think you've grasped his essence, his double appears behind you, smiling ironically, and you lose your hold on him.

This is not a moral tale. Which is why it must begin, in my telling of it, in a place where shadows still meet shadows and who you think you are can still be ambushed by who you've been all along: the casbah in Algiers.

1.

ALGIERS

The moment Oscar murmured to him: 'Dear, *vous voulez le petit musicien?*', and young André, his throat dry, paused, then hoarsely whispered '*oui*', something inside him fell *loose*. Every time he sought pleasure in later life, he said, it was the memory of that moment and of what came next that he reached for. More than that: 'ran after'.

It had taken just one husky syllable, a faint puff of air—*oui*—and the Devil had finally won. But it was Oscar Wilde who laughed out loud, as if he'd just caught the triumphant glint in the Wily One's eye. Not that Oscar believed in the Devil quite yet, although André, just twenty-five and fresh from Normandy, where everyone always said '*non*', not '*oui*', still did. Oscar laughed brazenly, unstoppably, Gide later wrote. He was still laughing as they rattled away down the hill in their fiacre.

All this is well-known. I've known it myself since I was fourteen.

The curious thing about this rendezvous in the casbah is that it almost didn't happen at all. The Devil won by a whisker. If, three days earlier, André had glanced to the left instead of the right as he paid his hotel bill in Blidah, he would not have ended up in the casbah in Algiers with Oscar Wilde that January night in 1895. If only he'd looked to the left as he stood at the desk in the foyer, there'd have been no strangled '*oui*', nothing would have loosened in him and come tumbling out—not then, at any rate, not in the way it did— and everything in his life would have fallen out differently. And I really do believe, in a funny sort of way, in mine as well.

♦

It was neither late at night nor January when I found myself sitting on a step, somewhere high up towards the top of the casbah, remembering Oscar Wilde. It was midday and early April. There were plenty of sensational historical incidents I could have brought to mind (the catalogue of invasions from the Phoenicians to the French is staggering), but instead I found myself recalling that singular moment—on the face of it so banal, so insignificant—when, somewhere near where I was sitting over a century later, André Gide had whispered '*oui*'.

Most of us will remember a moment such as this when we were younger: a jolt, a kaleidoscopic jiggling of memories and desires—and there we were, like André Gide, reconfigured, ready at last to have a life instead of just living. Had this ever happened to the men in blue pants and singlets hanging their bird-cages out in the sunny gap between the houses behind me? Would it one day happen to the small boys kicking a football around in the dust further up the hill?

I don't mean, by the way, those merely epiphanous moments we all experience from time to time—organ-music washing over us in a burst of joy in Notre Dame, for instance, or any of those sudden, soaring, symphonic moments when the mind is swallowed by the heart—surely everyone has those. No, I mean one of those moments when right out of the blue something (a word, a gesture) fits like a key into the clamp on our soul, unlocks it and throws it wide open, letting who we are come spilling out at last. At last we can start living out who we've been all along, at first in the shadows and now in the light.

I made a few nervous forays into the blur of my own memories to see if I could put my finger on such a moment in my own life—surely there'd been one—but I was weary from my steep climb and my eyes were full of the whiteness of Algiers, cascading down the hillside to the blinding sea beneath me like crushed lace. The moment refused to surface.

At the top of the casbah, high above the modern city strung out along the seafront below, it was quiet. At the bottom of the hill near the Ketchaoua Mosque, where I'd started my climb, Algiers had been a raucous bazaar, a blue and white checkerboard of streets and squares, choked with traffic, swarming with shoppers picking a path amongst the merchandise piled on the pavements. But in the casbah the ancient cobbled laneways were mostly too crooked and steep for cars, the doors to the shabby houses almost all shut. It had a deserted, half boarded-up feel to it. To tell the truth, once the boys had disappeared up the alleyway above the steps I was sitting on, all I could hear so high up was the tap-tap-tap of the shoemaker a little further along the lane. Taptap-tap—silence. Tap-tap-tap—silence. Nothing stirred.

To be honest, I'd been hoping for something more alarming than cobblers and canaries. The days of the *bagno* (the vast slave barracks of Algiers) were, of course, long gone. In those days thousands of enslaved Christian seamen, snatched by the corsairs, milled around in the taverns and eating places outside their barracks, raising hell and swapping tales of high adventure in China, Greenland and Mexico: captains consorted with cabin-boys, cut-throats with priests, titled Englishmen with whale-hunters from Denmark . . . it was such a roiling, roistering hotbed of life lived to the full that many refused to go home after being ransomed. Frenchmen in particular were rumoured to be ready to turn Turk—'to don a turban as easily as a nightcap'. At the very least, I'd hoped for swarthy men in turbans, glowering as I passed, veiled women vanishing silently into dark doorways as I approached. Perhaps it was more menacing at night. Not that I would ever venture into the casbah in Algiers at night these days.

Night. I wandered on, past the cramped, dark recesses in the walls where men sat playing draughts, having their hair cut and flapping at flies, and thought again of Oscar and André on that corner late at night a century or more before me . . . Oscar's large, white hand on André's shoulder, the whispered invitation, the booming English laughter, and then the clatter of wheels on paving stones as their fiacre wound down the hill towards the gas-lit boulevards below—and sin. That corner was probably just a stone's throw from where I was loitering in the sun in the rue Sidi Driss Hamidouche. The casbah of Algiers is quite small, after all, just an eyrie above the bay, a tight tangle of grubby streets and steps jammed between ancient walls on a sharp ridge, knifing up from the port.

They'd just left a nearby café where, squatting with cups of mint tea on a mat-covered platform, half-asleep in the fire-lit darkness, they'd been joined by a slender young man, scarcely more than a boy, wearing those white, ballooning breeches you now see only in paintings. Olive-skinned, with the languid eyes of a hashish-smoker, Mohammed, as he was called, sat down cross-legged on a stool below them and began to play quietly on a reed flute. The café fell silent. Soon the boy who'd served them their tea, the *caouadji*, came over and sat beside Mohammed, accompanying him softly on his goblet drum. It must have sounded like clear water trickling over sharp stones. And André's eyes lingered on the fluteplayer's supple fingers and slim, burnished legs. A Greek goatherd playing his flute. Time had evaporated. He was nowhere and everywhere, he was in a trance... he had forgotten who he was, until Oscar took him by the arm, jerking him back into the present. They went outside. And at the next corner, laying his pale, pudgy hand on his young companion's shoulder, apropos of nothing that had been said in the café that night, or in any other café anywhere else, for that matter, not even in Paris, where they'd met for many intense tête-à-têtes—apropos of nothing at all, Oscar Wilde whispered those startling six words. And after half a lifetime of saying '*non*', André said '*oui*'.

Yet what was so memorable about this episode? Why dwell for even a moment on a callow young Frenchman and an Irishman with bad teeth picking up boys together in Algiers one night in 1895? Strictly speaking, it wasn't even André's first time—not quite, although, admittedly, the other two times, in Tunisia and on Lake Como, hadn't *unlocked* anything in him. They'd dangled a key, perhaps, but never inserted it in any lock. Certainly nothing had come tumbling out.

As I made my way back down the hill towards the arcaded streets of the modern town, squashed between the bay and a wall of hills, I asked myself why it was *this* shadowy scene that I'd so vividly recalled on my walk through the casbah instead of... well, something of more consequence: the arrival of the first Roman legions, for instance, or the first wave of Vandals, or that marvellous moment in 1829 when the Dey of Algiers struck the French consul three times across the face with his peacock-feather fly-whisk, calling him a 'wicked, faithless, idol-worshipping rascal' (which he was), thereby provoking the French to occupy Algeria. Or, if it had to be an erotic moment, why not some celebrated love affair, something tragic and tumultuous, conducted beneath carved cedar ceilings picked out in gold and painted in vermilion? When all was said and done, this *was* Dido and Aeneas territory. (Well, not quite, that was next door in Tunisia, but almost.) Why not something epic, something extraordinary, rather than *this* unremarkable encounter?

Even what happened next in the rooms Oscar had rented somewhere down by the water (Oscar in the back room with the drummer, André in the front room with the flute-player) is common enough—practically clichéd. André's 'shuddering jubilation' and so forth, all that overheated business about 'what name shall I give the bliss I felt to be holding tightly in my naked arms that perfect little body, wild, fervent, lascivious and saturnine'—well, some version of all that has happened to almost everyone, surely. And as for André's soul and body being so light all the next day that he almost blew away—it's disarming, and stirs memories, but it's hardly momentous.

It was, it's true, a quintessentially *modern* moment. That is to say, it was above all André's psyche rather than his body that went adventuring that night in the casbah: he was exploring his own mind's labyrinths rather than the casbah's. This was an act of pure *self*-discovery, not a heroic quest to find the Northwest Passage or the source of the Nile; this was merely dallying with danger rather than a swashbuckling fight to the death with monsters or marauding natives. Dispiritingly, this sort of adventure is the only sort left to most of us now that there's virtually nowhere left for us to go—nowhere wildly unfamiliar—and absolutely nothing left to do when we get there except photograph it. No wonder it was Oscar Wilde who triggered it in André's case: he was so modern that he's still modern a century after he died. As André told his mother just two days before going to the casbah with him, Wilde was nothing less than 'the most dangerous product of modern civilisation'.

However, whether being the distilled essence of modernity is enough to make something memorable or not, I'm not sure. For instance, I had an almost identical adventure to Gide's in a tea-house in Tunisia not long before going to Algiers, yet it's already not much more than a spicy anecdote. Needless to say, there was no flute-player, slim and dark as a demon, sitting cross-legged on the stool at my feet—it was instead one of the merchants from the nearby souk: he sold those kid-leather slippers in garish colours that Tunisians seem to have a passion for—but I *was* sitting on a mat-covered platform just like Oscar and André, drinking mint tea. The merchant's name was Abdul and he was clearly smoothing the way towards making me a delicate offer of some kind. However, because of the frenzied Arab music coming from the next room where there happened to be a camel—a real, full-sized camel, festooned as if for a tribal wedding, drawing water from a well—I was slow to grasp what precisely it was that was being offered. Not wanting to watch this poor beast ceaselessly turning, turning, as it winched up the water, I'd headed for the smaller room to one side.

After the brilliant spring sunshine in the streets outside, it had seemed gloomy at first in this side room, but gradually my eyes took in the gleaming tiled walls and floor, the mat-covered bench on which young men lounged, silently watching, and the alcove where hookas were being prepared. I sank back against the wall to wait for my tea. It was siesta time in Kairouan.

Abdul was in no great hurry. He embarked on some long story about how the well in the next room was 'sacred', wondrously connected to the Holy Well of Zemzem in Mecca itself, if I understood him correctly, which in turn is said to flow directly from Paradise. Mixed with honey, he assured me with a smile I found difficult to interpret, the water of Zemzem has miraculous qualities.

'So,' I said, 'will our tea be made with this miraculous water?'

'What else?' His grin suited him. 'But it doesn't work for infidels.'

I wondered if the Baptists back at Sousse, where I was staying, might be interested in this story of the water straight from Paradise. Sousse is a beach resort town of no particular distinction, although popular with Ukrainians. Earlier that same morning I'd found myself having breakfast at my hotel with a large family of Baptists from Tennessee. Once the prayers and blood-curdling Bible readings were over (Psalm 59: 'O Lord God of hosts, the God of Israel, awake to visit all the heathen: be not merciful to any wicked transgressors . . . Consume them in wrath, consume them that they may not be'—and much worse) they'd exchanged a bit of chit-chat about what they would be praying for that day—for the sweetness of Jesus to come into the hearts of those they met and so on. Then the paterfamilias, reaching for the fig jam, turned to me and asked: 'And what is your prayer for today, my friend?'

'Ah, well,' I said, 'I'm going to Kairouan.'

'Kairouan!' He froze, knife immobilised in the jam. The whole table froze. 'Kairouan,' he said softly, looking me straight in the eye, 'is the heart of evil.'

This was thrilling news. I knew hardly anything about Kairouan, really. I did know that while passing through it on his first trip to Africa, just over a year before the incident in the casbah, Gide and his companion Paul Laurens were invited to a feast of thirty-two courses by the caliph, but I had no idea why. I also know that the vast Mosque of Sidi Oqba in Kairouan—the Great Mosque, as everyone calls it—is the fourth most important destination for pilgrims after Mecca, Medina and Jerusalem. It had probably been there that he'd witnessed believers dancing in a state of 'mystic madness' to the music of Negro drummers, beating on their tom-toms and long-drums under a 'downpour' of clacking castanets. Seven visits to the Mosque of Sidi Oqba are worth one to Mecca. Unfamiliar as I am with all the intricacies of divine bookkeeping, I presume, however, that no merit at all accrued to either André or me for visiting it.

A few years after the episode in the casbah, while passing through Kairouan again, this time with his wife Madeleine, Gide was smitten by a lithe, knife-thin young mountain goat of a boy, who laughed and kissed him on the lips. Later at the railway station, as they were leaving, this Mohammed (as he was inevitably called) tried to lure him, wife or no wife, into staying in Kairouan a little longer. Scenes of thwarted craving as the railway carriage pulled out of the station. Poor

André! What might have been can stay painfully with you so much longer than what actually happens. And there's something unnerving about railway stations in general, I think: all those tearful partings, all that edgy waiting to the sound of screeching trains, all those strangers eyeing each other shiftily, the smell of sweat and cigarettes, the seediness, the loitering. There's an unease, I find, a faint echo of anguish, about any railway station wherever it is. Or there used to be before they became huge shopping malls.

'We'll pray for you,' the Baptist said. The whole family—grandma, sons, daughters-in-law, grandchildren—nodded.

'I'd rather you didn't,' I said, 'it's not something I feel comfortable with.' I can't stand this sort of spiritual meddling. Nobody has the right to ask for favours on my behalf without my leave. I was on the point of adding that I had a bright blue Hand of Fatima up in my room, which I was sure would ward off evil just as effectively as the unasked-for prayers of Baptists from Tennessee. But I thought better of it.

'Aren't you a Christian?' The knife was still stuck in the fig jam.

'From your point of view,' I said, choosing my words carefully, and knowing I sounded pompous, 'probably not.' A distinct chill descended on the gathering, so, as soon as I could get to the fig jam, I ate up quickly and set off for the bus to Kairouan. The train unfortunately no longer runs.

By early afternoon, in the café with the camel, I was pleasantly fatigued. The race in the minibus across the plains from Sousse, past herds of goats and olive groves, with French rap music blaring from a ghetto-blaster had been enough to daze anyone. I'd admired the serene, cloistered vastness of the courtyard of the Sidi Oqba Mosque, almost deserted in the stark early morning light. I'd dutifully visited the tiled *zaouia* or tomb of Sidi el-Ghariani, in a room off a cool, colonnaded courtyard like a miniature mosque's. I'd picked my way through the maze of the medina with its crooked passageways hardly wide enough for a donkey to squeeze through, ending up at the souk near the ancient southern gate of Bab ech-Chouhada (perfumes, copper, ceramics, carpets, shoes, wedding delicacies and djellabas—nothing I wanted, but I lingered, let the men take me by the arm and coax me to make a purchase, just to pass the time . . . 'A handbag for your wife . . . A dab of this just *here* and you'll feel young again for hours . . . No wife? No friend? Let me be your friend'). It had been a tumultuous morning and I needed to sit down.

After we'd drunk our first glass of tea Abdul, my slipper-merchant friend, gleaming as if he'd come straight from the hammam, offered me first more tea, then an orange juice and then, not at all coyly, himself. Deftly switching roles and using more or less the same words as Oscar Wilde had in Algiers, he then offered me the waiter, who was indeed so languidly beautiful he could have slipped off one of the Roman mosaics I'd seen in Tunis. What about the lad in the electric blue djellaba lolling by the window, then? There was a kind of promising ductility about all of them. The game was played with a lightness of touch I couldn't help admiring. And it *was* just a game. Abdul was simply amusing himself during his lunch-break. The idea was that I should lose and pay up.

In a word, encounters of this kind, in themselves, whether or not they end in 'shuddering jubilation', are two-a-penny. The script might differ in its details according to the place and time, but in its general outline it's everywhere the same.

Yet those six words of Oscar Wilde's and André's hoarse '*oui*' still echo in my mind as if I'd been hovering there beside them that winter's night in 1895—and not just because Wilde and Gide turned out to be famous men, either. Their friendship was dotted with many other exchanges that nobody remembers at all. What makes these words and what followed so memorable?

I first read them at the age of fourteen standing up in the paperback section of a Sydney bookshop where I was working during the Christmas holidays. In those days the shelves were still made of wood and needed daily dusting. Feather duster in hand, I'd paused at the Gs on this particular morning, taken down an orange and white Penguin paperback entitled *If It Die* ('An uninhibited autobiography recording experiences of and reflections on French life from Gide's childhood to the eve of his marriage')—'uninhibited' . . . 'French life' . . . the dusting would have to wait—and, flicking through it, almost at the end, I came across the words I would never forget, translated into English: *'Dear, would you like the little musician?'* And in a 'choking voice' Gide said 'Yes'. A pivotal moment. At fourteen, just as you're learning to conceal your own burgeoning double life, it's thrilling to read about a young man ten years further down the track taking the first step towards laying his bare. Even at fourteen I knew a pivotal moment when I came across one.

◆

You didn't find yourself in a coffee house in the casbah with Oscar Wilde at midnight completely by accident. Chance played its part, but it wasn't like a flat tyre or getting struck by lightning. Isn't everything that happens a sort of double helix of the willed and unwilled, if you look closely enough? Even getting struck by lightning. In one sense Gide's pivotal moment was utterly willed. In fact, it was almost choreographed.

In going to the casbah with Oscar Wilde, Gide was asking for trouble. Wilde was a dangerous corrupter of youth. And that vicious mouth of his, reeking of absinthe, had been promising to suck young André's soul out of him for several years. To agree to go off with him like that to some louche den in the native quarter of Algiers was just begging to be debauched.

A few pirouettes for the Irishman's admiring eyes at one of Mallarmé's Tuesdays in Paris three years earlier—well, that was one thing, even if he was terribly white, this Irishman, an undulating caterpillar nibbling ever closer, nibble, nibble—although, as it happens, André had a passion for caterpillars. He had a passion for any insect, really, as well as the sort of creature you find in rock pools, but particularly for caterpillars. But going alone with him to the casbah late one night was something else entirely.

And he'd been warned, too. 'I want to teach you how to lie,' Oscar had told him during a private moment in Paris, when they first met, 'so your lips become beautiful and twisted like an ancient mask's'. Almost too Wildean to be believable, that line. But he did say it, apparently. Being Irish, and still a pagan at that point, he knew exactly where to stick a knife into a pious Protestant. It was ravishingly well aimed, a masterstroke of seduction at every level. 'You have no soul,' it said, 'a mask is all there is, and I will delight in twisting its thin, tight lips into a sinner's smile.'

In point of fact, André's face was already slightly mask-like at twenty-two, it was the eyes and cheekbones that did it, having a faintly Oriental cast to them. 'A hint of the Mongol', his friends called it, although this was nonsense: his mother Juliette Rondeaux was from

Normandy and the Gides, while originally of Italian stock, had been French for 400 years.

Regardless of any Mongol tilt, the young André was not beautiful or even particularly good-looking—not the kind of succulent morsel Wilde normally felt hungry for at all. '*Il n'était pas beau*', as people said of him, covering quite a range of physical possibilities in just one pouting syllable (*beau*). Remarkable eyes—'you listen with your eyes' Oscar once told him—but not remarkable enough to make him *beau*. If anything, at twenty-two he was a bit on the mousy side, despite the cape, the long hair and his strenuous attempts to appear interesting. Did he instead have the kind of face someone like Oscar Wilde might well think he could mould something beautiful out of? That, as we know, can ultimately be much more *interesting* than mere good looks.

It was also foolish of him to go with Wilde to that café that night because in Paris a few years earlier he'd nearly gone mad with Oscar Wilde. He'd felt violated by him, spiritually annihilated. 'Since Wilde I hardly exist at all', as he told the poet Paul Valéry, which would have been music to Oscar's ears: that we hardly exist—that there is no true face beneath the mask, no self to be true to—was precisely Wilde's point. André had to ward Oscar off like a diabolical familiar that winter of 1891–2. To cure himself of Wilde and to find his own true face, he'd fled south to Uzès (good Huguenot territory, the heartland of generations of Gides), plunging back into his Bible and showering God with pleas and promises. 'Lord, I return to Thee because I believe that all is vanity except knowing Thee. Guide me in Thy ways of light. I have been following twisted paths... I thought to enrich myself, but made myself poorer... O Lord, keep me from evil...'

On the very morning of his seduction, Wednesday, 30th January 1895, he dashed off a revealing letter to his 'sweet' mother before leaving for the casbah with Wilde. After lying to her about 'meeting up with Wilde by chance' and a few suspiciously rhapsodic lines on the beauties of Algiers (its blue-glazed walls and 'enchanted' streets, the shadows there 'even more mysterious than in the souks'—actually the weather was foul and getting worse, and young André was clearly getting himself overexcited), he mentioned the 'shudder of terror' he always felt in Wilde's company.

A few years later, once Wilde was dead, Gide wrote a rather touching memoir of him. Certain of Wilde's intimates, such as Robbie Ross, were much impressed by it. Here he professed to feeling 'affection, admiration and respect' for the great writer... well, he hadn't been so much a great *writer*, Gide wrote, as a great '*viveur*'. Some fine lines had flowed from Wilde's pen, in other words, but really it was his life which had been the great work of art. If anyone had the right to say this, Gide did, because it was to none other than the young Gide that Oscar had pithily remarked: 'I have put all my genius into my life, I've put only my talent into my works'. He now remembered Wilde as 'handsome', even 'radiant', like an 'Asian Bacchus', a Roman emperor, Apollo himself.

Although too flattering by half, these pagan allusions have a ring of truth about them: it was never evil which tempted Gide to stray from the Lord's paths of light, but paganism. Not just any kind of paganism, either, nothing Hindu, for instance, nothing Norse, not even the heathenish habits of the savages in Tahiti—none of that seems to have particularly excited him. Much more dangerously seductive than any of these things, and much more alluring than the blandishments of 'the Devil', was the idea of the lightly clad goat-herd with a pipe. God's real rival was Pan. Coincidentally, just days before meeting up with André with such well-known consequences, Oscar wrote a letter to Robbie Ross invoking precisely this kind of pagan fantasy. He and his floppy-haired lover Lord Alfred Douglas ('Bosie' to his intimates) had 'been on an excursion into the mountains of Kabylia' in Algeria, where the villages were 'peopled by fauns. Several shepherds fluted on reeds for us. We were followed by lovely brown things from forest to forest. The beggars here have profiles, so the problem of poverty is easily solved.' And once Mohammed had fluted for him so unforgettably in the casbah in Algiers, André found satyrs with laughing eyes, skipping about on their goatish hooves and blowing on their reeds, almost everywhere he went. Indeed, for the rest of his life, he almost never went anywhere he was unlikely to find them. From the age of twenty-three Gide travelled above all, it seems to me, in search of Pan. He travelled almost always—to Africa, Italy, even to Stalin's Russia (where he found fauns aplenty)—to escape from the Christianity which had formed him. Sometimes I suspect that I have done much the same thing—in much the same places. (It's an escape from something you feel a strong attachment for, in a curious sort of way, not something you hate.)

A century ago you were mostly likely to come across fauns and shepherds untainted by Christianity, or at least anything Gide or I would recognise as Christian, around the Mediterranean (North Africa, Sicily, Italy and, more distantly, Greece), the lands any educated young man would have formed a vivid picture of in the late nineteenth century from reading Virgil and Theocritus. Gide's Virgil was very well-thumbed. North Africa, Sicily, Italy: this is precisely the route he took on his first foreign adventure in 1893 (unless you count a brief trip to Spain with his mother seven months before). And this, with a cockiness which takes the breath away, was also the route he chose for his honeymoon with Madeleine three years later, but in reverse.

◆

However, in addition to toying with a fall, there was also an unwilled side to his casbah escapade. If Gide had just glanced to the left instead of the right in the hotel foyer in Blidah the previous Sunday he'd have ended up not in the casbah with Oscar Wilde, but far away across the mountains in Biskra. If it hadn't been for a fleeting attack of decency in Blidah, André would have taken the train to Biskra, as he'd planned, to write in the chilly sunshine for a while, on the northern edge of utter emptiness. How Oscar, prince of irony, would have roared with laughter if he'd known that, ironically, the puritanical young Frenchman had ended up indulging in lewd acts in a sleazy hotel in Algiers through a misplaced sense of decency.

People with no imagination call this sort of thing 'fate'. Such a lazy word, 'fate', almost meaningless—in retrospect anything at all can appear fated, anything you haven't consciously willed can be written off as fate or destiny. Or the stars or karma or the will of some god or other. You didn't choose on this occasion, you were chosen, so it was obviously meant to be. *Mektoub*, as the Arabs say—'it is written'. But by whom, exactly? And why on *this* particular occasion and not others? Why not when you were deciding whether or not to emigrate to Canada or choosing new wallpaper for the living room? Why now?

Gide himself would probably have called what happened in Blidah an example of *'inconséquence'*, the randomness or disconnectedness of things. Some things just happen in life, he'd have said (including, by his own admission, most of his books). He *might* have looked left in the hotel foyer—or at the ceiling or straight ahead—but, as it turned out, for no reason at all (perhaps a fly buzzed past) he looked to the right, setting off a chain reaction catapulting him into the casbah in Algiers. And ultimately setting off hundreds of millions of other chain reactions, one of which, by the late afternoon of that day in the casbah, had me sitting over a century later with a coffee on the terrace of the St George hotel in Algiers waiting for a man I'd never met called Yacoub.

◆

To pass the time while waiting for Yacoub to turn up, I tried jotting down a few of my own pivotal moments on the only piece of paper to hand: my grubby map of the city. My visit to the tea-house in Kairouan—the one with the camel and the gleaming slipper-salesman—was clearly not a pivotal moment. Life did not, in an ecstatic volte-face, turn to openly embrace my imagination, as Gide's had done in the casbah. In Kairouan I did not begin, as he did, on the corner of that lane with Oscar's hand on his shoulder—deliriously, by the way, without the slightest remorse—to live out who I'd really been all along. Where, if ever, had that happened? Eventually, on a pale blue expanse marked port d'alger,

I wrote 'Morocco'. I set my pen down on the map, which was by this time covered in comforting coffee rings, and let my mind wander. The café at the old St George is the perfect place to do that.

Cafés for me are the quintessence of travel. I don't mean to suggest that cafés are what travel is all about, but for me they're at the core of it. Travel is simply not travel without cafés. Restaurants, on the other hand, strike me as overrated. Unless the company eclipses all the tedious, time-wasting rituals of ordering and eating food in noisy surroundings, restaurants are all too often just hard work. Beaches, art galleries, cathedrals, museums of native crafts, Mt Everest at dawn, penguin colonies and all the other things whoever writes the tourist brochures seems to think we leave home to see can be diverting, relaxing, inspiring and even instructive in short bursts. Without cafés, however, they turn into an endless exhibition we have to trudge through, an interminable procession of panoramas and *tableaux vivants* we're obliged to inspect.

It's not the cafés themselves that are essential to travel. I don't much care about the ambiance or the quality of the coffee and cakes. It's the act of sitting down in them that's significant. Cafés are clearly perfect for conversation and dalliance, but, more importantly, they're where you put yourself back together again, changed but still you, after flying apart in the Prado or the Kalahari. They're where you remember who you're supposed to be. I know that's partly why I feel no desire at all to go to Antarctica, for instance. Ships on their way to Antarctica sail past my window every summer, I can watch them heading south from where I'm sitting now, yet I have not the slightest desire to go on one, my sail 'trembling with the violence of the spirit' (as Nietzsche said an adventurer's sail should) because between where I am sitting, at the bottom of Tasmania, and Tierra del Fuego on the other side of the globe, there is not a single café. I know Antarctica is a dangerous wonderland of glaciers and penguins, I know it's unlike any other landscape on earth, sublimely, terrifyingly, unimaginably beautiful, but in terms of cafés it's a wasteland. My kind of traveller needs oases.

That's why the terrace café at the old St George (or the Hôtel El Djazaïr, as it now calls itself—'more than a hundred years of experience, prestige and cordiality') strikes you as soon as you walk out onto it as being more than just somewhere you might sit with a drink: it's also an oasis. Every serious traveller knows the thrall and bliss of an oasis. It's in the traveller's (although not necessarily the holidaymaker's) blood: deserts of one kind or another fill your days and then you come to an oasis.

Since the St George is in the middle of Algiers, its oasis is fake. You make your way through a few rooms of faux Moorish opulence to the back of the hotel and there it is: a tiled terrace, complete with fountain, looking out on thickly planted, slightly bedraggled gardens dotted with Japanese businessmen taking photographs. It's really just a clutch of palm trees, cannas, cordylines and vines, but it's soothing after the long walk back from the casbah through the clamour of the city centre. In the pullulating streets down by the water—elegantly arcaded, Paris by the sea, but chaotic, a tumult of colour and sound, thronged with merchants and shoppers, overflowing with shoes, silver, spices, perfumes, djellabas, glassware, crockery, croissants, oranges, aubergines, bangles, brassware—my mind had been just a jigsaw of images in a wash of sound. Language had fled. This had been the landscape of forgetting.

On the terrace with my coffee and crumpled map, waiting for Yacoub, I felt language and memory trickling back. That's partly why I was sitting there, after all. I was waiting for Yacoub, certainly, but mostly I was remembering. Morocco. I went to Morocco when I was twenty-two, nearly the same age as Gide when he first arrived in North Africa with his artist friend Paul Laurens. It was the first utterly foreign place I'd ever been to. Although I didn't wander around the medina of Rabat in the moonlight, intoxicated with the perfumed, erotic foreignness of where I was, as Gide did when he first got to Tunis (there were no gold rings glinting in the darkness in Rabat, no bare feet on blue tiles), I did stay with an Arab family in a traditional, labyrinthine Arab house (with tiled courtyard and gallery—I thought I was dreaming) in the Arab quarter of Rabat. I did time-travel in the medieval laneways of Fez and Marrakech. And I did, like Gide, feel for the first time not so much the insincerity as the thinness of my fiercely eccentric religious self, and the stirring of another self. But was it a volte-face? Not quite. It was rather one link in a long chain, I told myself, beginning with that moment in the Sydney bookshop and ending here on the terrace of the St George Hotel. And Gide played a role in it: I went to Morocco in part because I'd read his autobiography as a boy, so going there was to some extent an act of remembrance, although I wouldn't have seen it like that at the time. It was also, as for Gide, leaving his Bible at home in France, an act of forgetting. One self was shunted off into the wings while a nervous second self, still blinking in the bright light, came out of hiding to take its first awkward steps around the stage. Like Gide, though, it was still very unsure of its lines.

In other words, it was time in Morocco to give an airing to the parallel life that reading Gide had hatched in me some years before. On the trip to Spain with his mother, the beauty of the Spaniards had 'hatched out' a shrouded self in the young Gide: '*j'éclos*', he wrote from Seville to a sympathetic friend, 'I'm hatching out', 'I'm bursting into flower ... the beauty of the people is driving me wild—as well as the smell of orange-blossom.' And one night in Moorish Granada, a gypsy boy singing a 'panting, unrestrained, painful song', his very soul expiring each time he ran out of breath, touched 'a more secret place in my heart', he wrote in his diary years later, than anything else had ever done—not even the songs of Egypt. And now, forty years after 'hatching out' and 'bursting into flower' in Morocco, driven wild by the beauty of the people—and the smell of spices in the souks, and the muezzins' chant—here I was, at the end of the chain, remembering André Gide in Algiers. And so remembering Morocco. And so, in its wake, more or less my whole life.

Morocco. Why Morocco? Why not Tunisia, say, or Egypt? Because ... because ... (and I began picking my way from Morocco back down the chain, link by link, looking for clues, inching towards the moment in the Gs in the Sydney bookshop when I was fourteen) ... there'd been St Exupéry, the famous aviator, Gide's friend, he'd written about Morocco and enchanted me when I was young ... and Paul Bowles, but had I even heard of him when I first went there? Or of William Burroughs, Alan Ginsberg, Truman Capote and the rest of that scandalous gang? *'Bonjour, Monsieur Dessaix! Yacoub ...'*

The tall, slim man who had appeared in the blink of an eye in front of me, extended a long arm with flamboyantly pink starched cuffs at the end of his sleeves to shake my hand. *'Désolé* about being late, but the traffic, you know—Algiers is just one big traffic-jam at this time of the afternoon.'

Morocco would have to wait.

Yacoub was a friend of a friend of mine in Paris, a Berber princess who knew every nook and cranny of Algiers. When we travel, we're prone to meeting up with friends of friends and the chance acquaintances of second cousins. Otherwise in a foreign city it's all too easy to feel you don't exist. 'If you go to Algiers,' Zaïda had said, 'you must meet Yacoub.'

'Who's Yacoub?' I'd asked.

'Ah! He's a poet, like you.'

'But I'm not a poet.'

'Nor is Yacoub, if you know what I mean.'

'Would Yacoub know anything about André Gide?'

'Yacoub knows a little bit about everything.'

I'd immediately felt very curious to meet Yacoub. 'And so tell me,' he went on, after we'd exchanged a few banalities, 'what are you doing in Algiers?' He used the intimate form (*toi*) as everyone in Algeria seems to do, even with total strangers, but it wasn't an entirely affable question. It never was in Algeria, starting at the airport.

'I'm here because of a caterpillar in Normandy' was the real answer, but that would have sounded flippant. 'I've been in Tunisia,' I said, 'so I thought I'd have a look at Algiers on the way home.'

'Uhuh,' he said, clearly intending to probe slightly deeper when the moment was right. 'And how do you like the hotel?' He was exactly as our friend Zaïda had described him, looking slightly *belle époque* in the late afternoon light—subtly striped suit, silk cravat, pocket handkerchief. Yet, for some reason I couldn't put my finger on, he looked a touch disreputable as well, like an ambassador to Paraguay who'd abruptly left the service under a cloud and settled in Belize. He ordered a Campari and soda and then glanced around the terrace to see who else might be there. The whine of a muezzin's call to prayer came drifting up the hill from the city, whisking me instantly back to Morocco where I heard my first muezzin, calling from a minaret just a few rooftops away in the early morning dark. I'd been so startled I'd stayed awake until dawn. The hotel. Did I like it. 'Well . . .' I began.

'No need to be nice about it,' he said, stretching his long legs out across the white tiles. 'It's state-run, of course—don't be fooled by all those touches of Oriental luxury. However hard they try, it still feels like Uzbekistan in the seventies, I always think.' He examined me briefly but quite intently across the table as if deciding how to play me. Lanky, with a touch of grey around the temples, he had those glistening black eyes you only see in North Africa.

'Were you in Uzbekistan in the seventies?' I asked. 'For a while, yes,' he said. 'In those days we were all socialists, you see. Naturally, I'd rather have been a socialist in Paris, who wouldn't? But one couldn't always choose.' He drummed lightly on the tabletop with his long, elegant fingers. 'In the old days this was quite the place to stay, you know—or at least to be seen. Churchill,

Eisenhower, the King of Greece, Edith Piaf.' It was hard to picture. At every table there seemed to be a stout businessman tapping away on his laptop or talking Russian into his mobile phone. 'Oh, yes. All the crowned heads of Europe, as it were. Simone de Beauvoir as well—she stayed here. André Gide . . .'

'Gide?'

'That goes without saying. Rudyard Kipling, the Rothschilds . . .' All of a sudden the old St George felt much less tired and much more glamorous. 'Not to mention Zaïda.' He smiled for the first time. A lean face, with a very fine jaw and chiselled cheekbones. 'How *is* Zaïda, by the way? Her message was so brief.'

Zaïda's messages are always brief, as if fired off backwards over her shoulder while she's busy with something more important. 'Fine, I think,' I began, trying and failing to catch the waiter's eye (it really *was* a bit like Uzbekistan in the seventies). 'To tell you the truth, I don't know her terribly well, we're sort of . . . well, it's a long story.' I meant that it was quite a short story, but that I wasn't going to tell it.

'Uhuh.'

'So Gide stayed here?'

'On his very first visit, if I'm not mistaken. Have you read any Gide?'

'As a matter of fact, I've just started rereading him—I've got his *Journals* with me at the moment—but I first read him when I was very young.'

Yacoub nodded. '*Fruits of the Earth*, *The Immoralist* and so on, I suppose.'

'Yes. And a few of the others as well over the years—the novels, *If It Die* . . .'

'So did I, it was part of growing up in those days, wasn't it. Not any more.'

'Why's that, do you think?' This could be tricky territory. I didn't really know Yacoub. 'Is he just out of fashion?'

'Too much pederasty and Christianity for modern tastes, I suppose, at least here in Algeria. Weren't they his two obsessions?' He turned away abruptly to intercept the waiter for me. 'Another cappuccino?' I nodded. 'Is that quite fair?' Was I defending André Gide or myself? I felt unexpectedly flustered, as if someone had cast aspersions on a close friend and so on me as well—on my judgement and affinities. Yacoub looked faintly amused, but not hostile. It was a look I was to encounter over and over again in North Africa. 'As it happens, I was thinking about Gide this afternoon. I took a walk through the casbah, you see.'

'Uhuh,' he said, adjusting his rather splashy cuffs. He gave no sign of making any connection between Gide and the casbah. He glanced at his watch. 'Would you like to go for a drive and see Algiers at sunset? We've just got time.'

'It's kind of you, but . . .'

'The basilica—when you've finished your coffee let

me take you up to Notre Dame d'Afrique. You can see halfway to Spain from there.'

As you certainly can. *Alger la Blanche* tumbles down the hillside beneath you to the vast bay, as white as fresh washing dipped in blue. Always white, like thousands of eggshells, like dunes of sugar poured from the sky. Then gradually, as we watched from the terrace in front of the basilica, *Alger la Blanche* turned ivory, amber, saffron and then vanished in an explosion of pinpricks of light. For a long time neither of us spoke. Then, as we wandered back to the car, Yacoub said: 'So why were you thinking of André Gide in the casbah?' I suspect he knew perfectly well why, but wanted to see what I might say. I began with what had happened in the hotel foyer in Blidah. He listened to me with that strange mixture of patient attention and utter indifference that comes over you when somebody else's child starts telling you about its day at school.

◆

On his second visit to North Africa, alone this time, André Gide was leaving Blidah early. Going to Blidah, *la petite rose*, just outside Algiers at the foot of the Atlas range in mid-winter had been a mistake: 'comfortable, well-managed and clean' (as a popular English guide described it) the hotel may well have been, but it clearly was not well-heated. Many Europeans spent the winter in Algiers: although not as warm as Madeira, it was the 'best winter residence within easy range of England', according to one British Ambassador from the period, and highly recommended for pulmonary complaints. Blidah, only a couple of hours away by train—nowadays it's really just an outer suburb of Algiers—was much colder.

Gide was miserable. 'The only leaves in your sacred wood,' he later wrote in his overwrought way, 'were those which spring does not renew ... The snow had come down the mountains close in to you,' he went on, 'I haven't been able to get warm in my room and even less so in your rainy gardens'. Blidah's gardens of olive trees, cedars and orange trees were just the place to dally in April, May and June, but not in January. In early spring, for instance, as one English guidebook noted, 'the air for miles around was perfumed with the scent of the orange blossoms'. In January Gide felt so dispirited that he started reading German philosophy, giving in gently to vague religious sentiments, never far from the surface when he was young, although already thinning. The faint sound of bugles wafting over from the French barracks pricked (agreeably, no doubt) at his mournfulness.

He stood it for three days and then decided to move on to Biskra. He was just paying his bill, his bags all loaded onto a carriage in the street outside to go to the station, when, glancing to the right, he noticed the names of the hotel's latest arrivals chalked onto a board: oscar wilde, lord alfred douglas.

On an impulse Gide quickly sponged his own name off the blackboard before setting off for the station. To be fair to André, it *was* 1895, the Marquess of Queensberry was closing in, and Oscar Wilde and Lord Alfred were not the kind of company one openly courted any more. Once at the station, however, about to get in the train, he had a fit of conscience. What if his old friends—and they *were* his old friends, he had to admit, even if he hadn't seen them for three years, unless you counted running across them briefly in Florence—what if they had seen his own name on the blackboard and now wondered why he'd left without knocking on their door? It would look crass. So he had his baggage put back in the omnibus and returned to the hotel. Since Oscar and Bosie were out, he sat down in the entrance hall to wait for them, his head in a volume of Dickens (*Barnaby Rudge*, of all things), which he knew would annoy Oscar. When Oscar eventually came in he was, it's true, not especially pleased to see him.

All the same, that evening the three of them went out on the prowl, looking for young men 'as beautiful as bronze statues', in Oscar's words, and finding none. Well, strictly speaking, André wasn't prowling, he was just tagging along. Any prowling double he might have had was still well cloaked and keeping its distance. At this early stage he was more inclined to fall in love with shadows than to prowl. He used to wander around Blidah, he said, and even further afield, 'looking at nothing and seeing everything' until his eye chose 'someone or something' to fall in love with. Oscar was not fooled for an instant by this sort of waffle.

In a café they were dining in later that evening a fight broke out between a group of Spaniards and some Arabs. Knives came out and the trio from the Hôtel d'Orient beat a hasty retreat. This was not the kind of *couleur locale* they'd been looking for. Blidah was proving a disappointment. When Oscar suggested meeting up in Algiers the next day, André said his first '*oui*'.

◆

This was about as far as I'd got with the story when we drew up at the St George—possibly a spot further, but I hadn't specifically mentioned *caouadjis* or flute-players, and certainly hadn't touched on shuddering jubilation.

'Would you like to drive down to Blidah tomorrow?' Yacoub said as he got back into his car. 'I don't think there's much to see there these days, but it's only an hour away. We could try to find this . . . what was it called? Grand Hôtel d'Orient.'

'I'm not on a pilgrimage or anything, you know, Yacoub,' I began. I hoped he wasn't jumping to conclusions.

'You're looking for *something*, I think. How about

I pick you up about ten?' That knowing smile again, which I couldn't fathom at all. It was friendly, mocking, playful and sincere all at the same time. But I wasn't *looking* for anything, I was waiting to be ambushed. There's a difference. Before I could toss this back at him, though, he leant across, wound down the window and said to me: 'And remember: if you're dining here tonight, *méfie-toi des petits musiciens* . . . definitely not to be trusted.' And off he drove. What a nerve! Forget any 'little musicians'—the one I shouldn't be trusting was Yacoub.

2.

BLIDAH

While Blidah is quite pleasantly situated at the foot of the Atlas Mountains just south of Algiers, it was hard to imagine what had brought people like Wilde and Gide in such numbers to this small town of no distinction a century ago. Driving around its traffic-clogged streets with Yacoub the next day, gazing slightly forlornly out of the window at the usual modern jumble of concrete and bricks, I couldn't see why the moneyed classes of France and England would choose to come here rather than, say, to some charming village in Italy or Spain. Although it was April, I could see nothing to suggest the town of petal-strewn paths and lilac groves full of birdsong that Gide claimed to have found when he returned to it in the spring after a spell in Biskra. There are no Roman ruins in Blidah, either, although the Romans did have a military station here two thousand years ago, and no thermal baths. There is no mysterious medina to get lost in, no casbah or citadel, no souk smelling of aniseed and cinnamon, awash with colour like a Delacroix canvas, not even a mosque worth more than a glance. We both fell silent in the rising heat as we drove around fairly aimlessly, hoping to chance on the Grand Hôtel d'Orient.

'To be fair,' Yacoub said, breaking the sticky silence, 'the old city, the Turkish city, was destroyed in an earthquake—just before the French got here, as I remember. So you mustn't expect too much.' He examined the modern blocks of flats we'd come to a standstill in front of, thrumming on the steering wheel. 'It's all rather square and French, isn't it.'

'It was a Turkish city?'

'Yes, the Ottomans were everywhere except Morocco. Didn't they teach you that at school in Australia? And before that it was an Andalusian city—a lot of Muslims from Spain settled here. Spain's so close. In fact, I think it was the Andalusians who planted the first orange trees.'

'So what on earth would people like Oscar Wilde and André Gide have come here for, do you imagine? It can't have just been the orange groves.'

Yacoub shrugged. 'To admire the squadrons of French cavalry? The finest Arab stallions in North Africa? I don't know.' In point of fact, Yacoub seemed to know quite a lot about many things, if pressed. It was how to press him that was tricky. I'd asked him during the drive what he did for a living, but all he would admit to for the time being was 'dabbling in a bit of journalism'. I doubted that the odd newspaper column would have paid for those onyx cuff links and Italian shoes.

Whatever the attractions of the barracks and stud farms for some, by the late nineteenth century they must have also been coming here partly to meet each other in the sun. Oscar said as much. 'I'm fleeing art,' he told André with his usual theatricality when they eventually met up that January day in 1895. 'I don't want to adore anything but the sun any more.' His duty to himself, he said, was to 'enjoy myself terribly' and that was best done mindlessly in the sun, his theory being that 'the sun detests thought'. The sun had eventually banished serious thinking, he assured his young companion, from wherever it had once flourished (Egypt, Greece, Italy, France and so on). Thinking was now possible only in Norway and Russia, where the sun, and he himself, never ventured.

Wilde wasn't just being camp, by the way. He knew precisely what he was saying and to whom. Exactly three years before, after several weeks of Oscar's company in Paris, the weeks that had nearly given him a nervous breakdown, sending him scurrying south to hide away and talk to God, André had written in his diary: 'Wilde, I believe, has done me nothing but harm. *In his company*

I forgot how to think. My emotions were more varied, but I forgot how to bring order to them ... I sometimes had a few thoughts, but I was so awkward in getting them moving that I felt forced to give them up.'

Apart from the sun, the famous orange and olive groves and the thick forests of cedar, there were also plantations of chestnuts and figs in Blidah to wander in. Indeed, according to Sir Robert Lambert Playfair's detailed guide for discerning tourists, there were 'charming promenades in every direction', as well as horse rides and long walks in the foothills behind the town. Those bent on killing wild animals, as the English and French often are, could slaughter panthers, gazelles and even lions if they ventured far enough into the mountains, as well as the usual partridges and bustards in season.

In short, Blidah offered you the Orient without putting you to the trouble of going all the way to Constantinople or up the Nile to find it. By the 1890s you could get there from London in four days via Marseille. It was, in addition, picturesque, had a sprinkling of the best people in the warmer months and, for those who wanted it, an agreeable whiff of vice. The whole city stank of hashish when Gide first visited it.

Towards midday, after luring an idle taxi-driver into our car with promises of a generous tip, we found the Grand Hôtel d'Orient on the corner of the Place d'Armes and a dark, narrow side street. Even Yacoub looked pleased. It's still clean, in a dingy kind of way, and quite possibly well-managed, but it is by no means the Savoy. It's almost impossible nowadays to picture Oscar Wilde, let alone all the other upper-crust visitors from London and Paris who stayed there, roaming with any dignity its yellowish tiled corridors or sharing bathrooms. These days, we gathered, arrivals of any kind are few. And the blackboard in the foyer is long gone.

It's not until you throw open the shutters in one of the bedrooms overlooking the small square, flooding the room with southern light, that you glimpse something of what must have drawn Gide and Wilde and quite a bevy of the well-born and well-heeled to Blidah a hundred years ago or more. If there were a church in one corner of the square, it could be in Spain. Yellow walls baking in the sun, blue-grey shutters, carpets being aired on narrow balconies. The people in the square, which is arcaded, almost like the courtyard of a great mosque, are strolling or sitting about in the sun with that particular mixture of indolence and edginess you rarely encounter in northern Europe. It has what Gide called '*grâce*'—graceful charm—together with something sharper, more troubling, like a half-hidden blade. The hills, which rise suddenly directly behind the square, dotted with villas, were a brilliant green the day we were there, as if painted onto the sky. Sometimes Gide went walking there, 'looking at nothing and seeing everything', presumably, and waiting for his eye to find 'something or someone' to fall in love with. Randomly. *Au hasard.*

We stood side by side in the window and let the view cast its spell. It was a temptation to stay there until evening, watching the mood of the square change with the shifting light. After lunch at one of the cafés below us I'd thought of trying to talk Yacoub into setting off into the mountains to the south towards Médéa and the desert. 'Ah, yes, *la ville d'abondance*, as the Ottomans called it,' he'd said, as if trying to remember Médéa more clearly. How did he know these things? ' "If evil enters in the morning, it leaves in the evening." That's what they said about Médéa.' But he hadn't been inclined to go there, fearing, perhaps, that evil might have entered the 'bounteous city' that morning and not yet found its way out.

They can have what is to me a strangely *embodied* sense of evil sometimes, the Arabs. (A bit like Tennessee Christians, as it happens.) I'd recalled the poor black goat that Gide had watched somewhere in North Africa being dragged through the streets to be slaughtered. As it passed each house the 'evil spirit' resting on the doorstep would enter the goat, which was draped in jewels and luxurious stuffs, and 'disappear'. And in Biskra, too, he once watched Arab women in a courtyard dancing in a frenzy to the beat of drums around a copper dish filled with water. While an old Negress, a sorceress, beat on the rim of the dish with a stick, the women undid their long hair and whipped the water with it. Once the demons that possessed them had been drawn down into the water and drowned, the dish was emptied in the street. Unable to stand it any longer, feeling they'd been caught up in the women's madness he and—well, I suppose it was the Algerian boy Athman he was always with in Biskra—fled. Athman must have been out of his mind with terror: he not only believed in demons, he believed that any kind of music was the work of the Devil himself, except for the sounds of a particular tortoise-shell viol with two strings. If you believe in the personification of goodness, I suppose it's a short step to believing in the personification of evil.

We stayed where we were at the window for quite a while, watching the bluest shadows I've ever seen creep out of the alleys and doorways to drown the square.

♦

'Tell me, why are you really here?' We'd just finished dinner in one of the cafés on the square. It was just warm enough to sit outside. The waiter was taking his time bringing the coffee. Yacoub spoke with his accustomed world-weariness tinged with mischief and, as usual, he was annoyingly difficult to read.

Well, I thought, why is anyone anywhere? Why are you sitting late at night on a square in Blidah, for God's sake, with a middle-aged Tasmanian you barely know? But I knew what he meant. More or less.

'It's a long story, Yacoub.' And this time it really was.

'Isn't there a short version?'

'Well, the short version would start with a caterpillar.' This did not surprise Yacoub in the slightest. 'It's because of a small, black caterpillar that I'm here right now having dinner with you—although the caterpillar is only the last link in a long chain of...'

'Tell me more about this magic caterpillar. *Elle m'intéresse, cette chenille noire.*' There's something much silkier and more suggestive about it when you say it in French.

The Caterpillar and the Castle

One cold Sunday afternoon a year or two ago, on a back road in Normandy, Zaïda the Berber princess stopped her car so that the three of us could stretch our legs. We'd been singing old Cole Porter songs to cheer ourselves up after lunch in a depressingly jolly restaurant by the sea. We'd tried Charles Trenet, but Miriam, the Sri Lankan artist from Melbourne, had wanted something 'a touch saucier', so we'd launched into 'Always True to You in My Fashion' and just kept going.

The restaurant had been full of large Norman families smelling of cider, tucking into bowls of steaming mussels in rich sauces at large round tables. No couples, no solitary diners with hungry eyes, just families. There are few things more depressing than gatherings of other people's families. 'Families—I hate you!' as the Oscar Wilde character in Gide's *Fruits of the Earth* famously exclaims, 'your enclosed hearths, your tightly shut doors, your jealously guarded happiness'. In that youthful work Gide still thought in his giddy way that he could escape them. To tell the truth, not just this restaurant but the whole of Normandy struck me as rather grim—beautiful, admittedly, in a green, sodden sort of way, but closed-off, as if peopled entirely by sanctimonious widows, priests and secret poisoners.

Admittedly, the spot where we chose to stretch our legs seemed almost enchanted. It was in a shallow, wooded valley in the Calvados region, with a meadow of buttercups sloping down towards a nearby stream. The hum of insects in the air, the quiet chirruping of hidden birds, somehow made the cool, greenish silence even thicker. An abandoned farmhouse just above us on the hillside seemed to be staring at us with suspicion. Nothing moved. *'Tout est mollesse et luxe,'* Gide once wrote about this part of Normandy, meaning that nature here was sumptuously soft, so soft that it induced a kind of lethargy unknown in the rocky, hard-edged south where his father's family came from. The Calvados was sleeping heavily that Sunday afternoon. You could almost hear its snores.

Then the princess (in jeans—she's an utterly modern princess) noticed a small, black caterpillar inching its way across the road right in front of our car.

If we'd stopped a second later, we'd have squashed it. We crouched to admire it. Shuffle, shuffle—so tiny, so tender. And it was headed for a gateway we'd hardly noticed on the other side of the road. The gateway itself was overhung with huge, old trees—holm oaks, perhaps—and half obscured by vines. On one wall was a small plaque: teau oque bai. I went over and pushed back the tangle of leaves to read it. It was the château de La Roque-Baignard. I was thunderstruck.

'Gide,' I said. 'La Roque-Baignard.'

'Who?'

'Gide, André Gide—he lived here as a child. This is his castle. This is where he spent his summers and started writing. Even after he married...' And my mind flew backwards, trying to gather up all the tiny, brightly coloured shards that Gide had scattered about in his books, books I barely remembered, then just a jumble in my memory. 'And he loved caterpillars,' I added.

'Then it's a sign,' said Zaïda the Berber princess gravely.

'*De bon augure, ça c'est sûr,*' said Miriam, whose French is never less than elegant. A sign, yes, but of what? Apart from anything else, I don't believe in signs. Who sends them? 'I wouldn't call it a castle, though,' she went on, in her precise, Sri Lankan way, peering through the trees at the small, pinkish, two-storeyed building with blue-grey shutters. 'It's more of a château.'

'But I'm sure it had a moat. That round tower with

the pointed roof—it's sitting in a moat, isn't it?' Moats and towers with roofs like witches' hats—that's what you want in a castle.

'No, I think it's just a pond,' said Zaïda, who was the tallest of us. She ducked under the barbed wire by the roadside and waded through the buttercup-strewn grass towards it to get a better look. I was afraid that the châtelain might throw open a window and start firing a blunderbuss at her. Neither Miriam nor I could drive. How would we get back to Paris? When she disappeared from view for a moment down by the gurgling stream, we both listened nervously for the baying of hounds.

'It's tiny,' Zaïda said with a big smile when she got back to the road, 'but straight out of a fairytale. It *is* a moat. It's hard to believe it's real.'

For that matter, it's hard to believe it's real when you read about it in *If It Die*, the book I chanced on at fourteen: the miniature château on its tiny island, the waterfall, the 'rivulet flowery with forget-me-nots', the flocks of swallows 'splitting the azure' with their cries, André as a boy fishing for trout; even years later you remember it, however vaguely, as an enchanted land. And one thing I never forgot: young André's disenchantment when he found that the nearby forests did not go on forever! He'd found their boundaries on an ordinance map. Now that was the perfect metaphor for something.

Before setting off again we looked for the caterpillar but it had gone.

'André Gide . . . remind me,' Zaïda said as we got back into the car. 'I mean, obviously I read something of his when I was at school, but I can't remember much about it. Or him.' It's a common problem. For some reason his works don't stay with you. They don't, as one of his friends and admirers wrote, become 'constant companions' as Chekhov's plays or a Jane Austen novel might. You remember vividly having been impressed, but can't for the life of you remember what it was that impressed you. Of all that I'd read over the years I had no sharp memory of anything except 'Dear, *vous voulez le petit musicien*?'

As we tried to make our way out of that lost valley (a *vallon* in French, which is more closed-in, more intimate than a mere valley) getting even more lost in the process, I scrabbled about in my memory, trying to patch together a picture of Gide. Protestant childhood, a spot of *volupté* in North Africa, marriage to Madeleine, a journey to the Congo, endless escapades with *garçons* all over the place from Morocco to Moscow, the names of a few of his books (*Fruits of the Earth, The Immoralist, The Vatican Cellars, The Counterfeiters*—'No, no, it was something else we read . . .' '*La Symphonie pastorale*?' 'That's it. There's a blind girl in it. Switzerland.' Precisely.)

What I didn't say, because it wasn't uppermost in my mind at that early stage, is that La Roque-Baignard was where André Gide became aware of leading a double life as his childhood fell apart. He puts it more poetically, naturally, in *If It Die*: he says that in later years, returning from his travels, he could 'appreciate the blanketing charm of the valley', whereas 'at the age when a surfeit of desire was swelling in me I was chiefly aware of its narrowness'. He was thinking, no doubt, of the time he was caught at school in Paris, scarcely ten years old, *not* living a double life: he'd been sitting happily on his bench enjoying in turn his 'pleasure' and some chocolates left over from dinner the night before. He was immediately whisked off by his parents to see a doctor who, pointing to a display of Tuareg spears on his wall, said that, if he didn't mend his ways, 'those are the instruments we will have to resort to, those are what we use to operate on little boys like you!' Post-Freud, we might wonder if North African tribesmen's spears were the wisest thing to threaten such an impressionable youngster with.

Trying to recollect André Gide as we drove towards Paris was like scraping the dust and sand of decades off a mosaic floor to uncover a half-forgotten face, barely remembered limbs. Some of the pieces seemed to have been broken or to have disappeared, but bit by bit a familiar image began to appear ... gladiators and gazelles, as it were, and rosebushes, cupids, cowherds, a naked youth playing a lyre ... the usual things you find in a mosaic, every image needing some background to make it look real.

The longer I talked—we must have been halfway to

Paris by the time I fell silent—the more strongly I felt that I was renewing a valued friendship I'd unaccountably let slip. More than that: I was restoring a lost intimacy. It was foolish of me, really, to give in to this surge of sentimentality in the gathering dark. I was just one of Gide's millions of readers, he'd only ever spoken to me through the black and white squiggles on the pages of his books. I really knew almost nothing about him, so we could hardly be friends. Intimacy was out of the question, it was like loving Jesus, it was absurd. But still, that's what it felt like.

'The thing is,' Miriam finally said, lilting very fetchingly, 'you make him sound a bit like you.'

'No, not at all,' I said, 'I don't mean to compare myself with André Gide at all.'

'I'm not talking about *comparing*,' she said, looking straight ahead at Paris, glowing like Gomorrah on fire in the distance, 'I'm talking about things shared.' At this, she glanced over her shoulder at me from the front seat, very briefly. 'You really must try to remember more of what he meant to you. And it sounds to me as if remembering him will be almost the same as remembering yourself.'

'Well, what *I* think,' said Zaïda, who is a compulsive traveller, 'is that you should go to Algiers, go to the casbah, go to—where was it? Blidah, Biskra—go to Tunisia, the Congo...'

'Well, I don't know about the Congo,' I said, 'the

Congo sounds a bit radical, but Uzès is not out of the question.' They both agreed that Uzès was a gem. The south, Languedoc, the sun, the rockiness, the *garrigue* (the scrubby hills to the west of Nîmes)—balm to the soul, it was almost Africa. So unlike Normandy. 'With goatherds everywhere you look, I should think,' said Miriam.

'And if you go to Algiers,' Zaïda went on, 'you must meet Yacoub.'

◆

It was just as well we'd stayed where we were, Yacoub and I. As it turned out, Islamists had stopped a taxi just outside Médéa that day and slit the throats of everyone in it. 'To keep the government on its toes, I suppose', Yacoub muttered when he read about it in the paper the next morning. Unshaven, he looked a bit like a bandit himself.

Most of the way back to Algiers we hardly spoke. Motorways numb the brain. Yacoub had found a barber before we left and was looking sleek again in that slightly dissolute way of his. Green, rolling hills, orchards, outcrops of high-rises like fortresses. No hint of the marshes that were there when the French first arrived or of their choking, swampy exhalations, virulently poisonous, which mercilessly cut off both young and old with 'wasting ague and malignant fevers'. 'Death-fraught' was the grim word one English visitor came up with to describe the plain between Algiers and Blidah not so many years before Gide's first visit. It would have been a good description of the area not long before my own visit as well, but not for pestilential reasons.

'And now tell me,' Yacoub said without looking at me, when we finally pulled up at the entrance to the St George, '*sans* caterpillars this time, why are you *really* here in Algeria?' Was he a spy or something? Was that why he was so *silky*? Or, having read Edward Saïd, did he just suspect that I was there for some disreputable Orientalist reason—to salivate over the exotic Arab 'Other', for instance, ravish it and then jet off home? Saïd's views are looking pretty one-sided, not to say wrong-headed, these days where I come from, but in Algeria they must seem right on target.

How tempting it was to give the Gidean answer: 'Because I knew I'd find myself interesting here.' But this sounds narcissistic to the uninitiated and in any case suggests another question: why?

Actually, those weren't quite Gide's words. What he wrote in his diary in 1896, wondering why he felt so bored in Rome (St Peter's, the Sistine Chapel and the Baths of Caracalla notwithstanding) was around the other way: 'I've found the secret of my ennui in Rome: I don't find myself interesting here.'

He did not, by the way, find himself uninteresting in the Capitoline Museum in Rome: there he was much taken with the small bronze *Spinario* (*The Boy with a Thorn in His Foot*). Although he'd no doubt many times seen pictures of this naked boy trying to get a thorn out of his foot, he was enchanted by the bronze itself, smooth and black as jasper, the small, bent body gracefully slender. He always found graceful slenderness—*gracilité* in French: it makes you think of swans—eye-catching, even heart-snatching on occasion.

Tellingly, this was the word he used to describe Mohammed sitting down cross-legged to play his flute for him in the casbah in Algiers, his bare foot also coming to rest on his bare knee. Unsurprisingly, this was also the word that sprang to mind when he described the night he spent with a young man called Ferdinand Pouzac, with whom he did eventually recapture 'the same euphoria, the same joyful rejuvenation' that he'd felt after his night with Mohammed in Algiers. (It had taken him twelve years.) As a matter of fact, in his memoir of this second night of delirium (a hot night in the countryside near Toulouse), he explicitly compared Ferdinand to the *Boy with a Thorn in His Foot*. Ferdinand was much older, naturally—in life, as opposed to art, Gide was not smitten with the *gracilité* of beardless little boys—but had the same *gracilité*. As they abandoned themselves to love, the farm boy's warm, tanned skin shining silvery grey in the moonlight, Ferdinand began to coo like a frenzied dove. Gide remembered him forever as his Woodpigeon.

But how to answer Yacoub's question about why I was there? I was there, as always, when I travel anywhere, both to forget and to remember—the very same thing, sometimes. Algiers was simply the right place at that time to do those two things. But that would have taken much too long to explain, especially at the entrance to the St George Hotel with the bellboy hovering. And especially to Yacoub. I still hadn't quite worked out who Yacoub was. Even after spending all those hours with him, I still wasn't quite sure what game we were playing or what the stakes were. In North Africa two strangers who are still sizing each other up always seem to be playing some game or other, each intent on cheerfully duping the other.

'When I've worked it out, Yacoub,' I said, 'I promise I'll tell you.' I had the distinct impression he'd make sure I kept my promise.

3.

TORNAC

How could I have told Yacoub about what had happened in Tornac? Yet what happened there cast considerable light on why the boy dusting the Gs in a Sydney bookshop ended up getting out of his car at the St George Hotel in Algiers fifty years later.

Just like Gide setting off for Uzès to escape Oscar Wilde and recompose himself, I'd set off for the south almost immediately after encountering the caterpillar at La Roque-Baignard, and for much the same reason. Needless to say, I hadn't been fleeing any insidious seducer—at my age they're distressingly thin on the ground—but I had felt a need to collect myself somewhere warm with red-tiled roofs where the breezes smelt of Africa, somewhere I could dust off that mosaic of André Gide. The dry foothills of the Cévennes seemed perfect. So, passing through Paris, I scooped up my young friend Daniel and headed south. Or, strictly speaking, since he was doing the driving, he scooped me up, from just outside the Monoprix on the rue du Temple. That's where Daniel always picks me up.

Travelling with a young companion can be exhausting, like struggling with a kite in a high wind for days on end, but it can also be exhilarating for the same reason. Gide never went anywhere without one. It's the tethering that's crucial: they must have enough freedom to soar and swoop, but to fall back to earth close by when the wind drops. It can be tricky.

To tell the truth, I'm never quite sure what cross-generational friendships are supposed to achieve. By and large, for instance, the young don't want to be mentored, Socratic services are not what they're looking for: if they want to know something, they'll Google it, thank you very much. And by and large I don't feel rejuvenated and refreshed by spending more than twenty minutes with youngsters who haven't got beyond life's base-camp, yet think they have the whole world figured out. I just feel tired. Now and again I've come across an exception: someone who never felt he belonged in the base-camp, someone who has gone adventuring on his own since his earliest years, searching out secret places where he can be good and beautiful in his own way. When I do chance on someone like that, I sometimes find myself taking what Gide called 'a sudden and violent liking' to him, startling both of us. It mellows with time. Daniel was like that.

Anyway, whenever I'm in Paris, I ring Daniel and suggest getting out of the city for a day or two, he shows a flicker or two of interest, preferring as he does to approach everything from an oblique angle, and then—abracadabra—he materialises in his old blue Peugeot in the rue du Temple and off we sail. We bicker amicably at first about anything, really: movies, global warming, head-scarves, the Dalai Lama. Then we reach a level of intimacy where we don't feel obliged to say anything at all.

We thought of staying at Uzès ourselves when we first set out. It was my idea, really, it seemed the obvious choice. Languedoc: more Latin than Normandy, as Gide said himself, rockier, harder, hotter, somehow older, as if the Greeks had just left, all pinks and greys and olive-greens, thrumming to the metallic sound of cicadas in early summer, 'a land of lucid poetry and beautiful severity'. And at its heart Uzès. If we felt like improving ourselves, Nîmes and its Roman ruins were just over the horizon and the Popes' Palace at Avignon was a hop, step and jump away. But when we got there, the narrow, stony laneways and tiny squares of Uzès were bursting at the seams with drifts of foreigners, its restaurants crammed with pink northerners noisily eating and drinking for want of anything better to do. Besides, said Daniel, it was all hopelessly *chichi*—'just a hotbed of high-class huckstering, really', as he put it—although he thought it might be more to his taste in winter. I rather liked it. Apart from anything else, I loved the pale turquoise shutters on all the houses and talked Daniel into buying an elegant pale turquoise sweater in a very *chichi* boutique on the Place aux Herbes.

Seized by the urge to get a feel for the town where young André had spent so much time as a boy, I suggested trying to track down exactly where he'd come to holiday with his uncle, but Daniel adopted his put-upon look and said: 'Why?' On the spur of the moment I couldn't think of a good answer. So we went back to the Gide Parking Station near the Bishop's Palace, got back into the old Peugeot and stared through the windscreen. That's when I thought of Albert. A short drive away to the west, in the small village of Tornac, beside a stream on the edge of a forest, lived an old friend of mine, Albert. Alone. In a very big house. There is nothing remotely *chichi* about Tornac.

'*C'est qui, Albert?*' Nonchalant but snappy, as usual. A pale turquoise sort of question, as a matter of fact. He was looking very fetching in his new sweater. I don't deny the pleasure of being in the company of someone who looks fetching.

'Oh, I've known him for years. He's from Pondicherry.' Daniel, who was hovering at the time on the edges of something Himalayan (Hindu, Buddhist—he refused to be tied down to names), didn't say anything, but I could tell he thought that this sounded promising. India. Pondicherry was nowhere near the Himalayas, of course, but still—it was India.

'Is he gay?'

'No, he's got ex-wives dotted about all over the place, as a matter of fact. You're quite safe.' In point of fact, Daniel was never *quite* safe. It was part of his appeal. 'Owns a bookshop. I think you'd like him. How about I give him a call?'

I had no doubts about Daniel liking Albert. His whole house (an old silk factory he'd renovated himself) was like a miniature Hindu temple, sweet-scented, aglow with small lamps scattered amongst the graceful figurines. What I doubted was whether Albert would take to Daniel: he'd always been completely frank about having little time for the young. *'Je déteste la jeunesse,'* was how he usually put it, which is somehow both more brutal and more abstract than any English equivalent. He was partly being provocative, but he also partly meant it: he found young people too tongue-tied and awkward to be bothered with. I was anxious that he might find Daniel not young enough to be enchanting, yet not old enough to be really interesting.

I needn't have worried. From the moment Albert opened his blue front door to us looking spry and birdlike in his creamy silk short kurta, I knew it was going to be all right. Daniel instantly put on his demure but alert look, which would disarm anybody. Pondicherry wafted out to envelop us—sandalwood with just a hint of curried fish—contrasting intriguingly with the counter-tenor singing Handel somewhere in the cool depths of the house. 'Come in, come in,' Albert said, kissing me in that *pouf-pouf* French way on both cheeks and shaking Daniel's hand. He could hardly wait to enjoy the wayfarers that fate had cast up at his door, even if one of them was on the wrong side of thirty. Albert, I must say, does adore happenstance.

Where it was that I first met Albert I can't clearly recall. It had something to do with walking groups—I do remember that. He was a member of one of those walking groups that seem to flourish among the inhabitants of Languedoc. Every few weeks bands of locals with a sprinkling of retired English vicars, Dutch piano teachers and the odd New Zealand potter set out for the day along walking paths through the countryside, usually enjoying a splendid lunch along the way. Albert is too frail to indulge in long hikes these days, some malady from his Pondicherry days having apparently flared up again in recent years; he rarely walks further than the empty monastery across the stream, or at most as far as St Baudile's, the abandoned Catholic church on the other side of the vineyard. He likes to make sure it's still shut, he says, but not because he's remotely Protestant. It was on these hikes some years ago, I think, that he became friendly with some Canadian friends of mine from Anduze, they took me to visit him in his bookshop, where he sat surrounded by piles of volumes on esoteric philosophies and Oriental bric-à-brac, and one thing led to another. Nowadays I rarely go to the south of France without at least calling in to see him. It's always a treat.

That first evening, when we finally got there from Uzès, I could hardly wait to slip off alone for an hour or two to wander along the road in front of his house. It's one of my main delights when I stay with Albert. After a day on French roads in Daniel's old Peugeot I wanted to sit somewhere quiet for a while—somewhere beside the stream that burbles past Albert's house, under the almond willows, with nobody but the jays and blackbirds for company. If I were lucky, I might even glimpse a kingfisher swooping low above the water, lustrous and lethal, like a bolt of vengeance.

The dirt road passing his house stands perched on the threshold between two worlds. On one side of the road, beyond the stream it meanders alongside, the fields and vineyards stretch out open to the sky all the way to the horizon; on the other side, half-a-dozen paces from the renovated barn I usually sleep in, abruptly, with no warning hillocks or undulations, stands the first wall of the Cévennes, covered in a thick forest of oaks, chestnuts and birches. Up in there lie hidden valleys, ruined castles on crags, paths leading nowhere and stony-faced villages where time has congealed. At Albert's gate you can literally stand with a foot in both worlds. We'd no sooner stepped from the car than I was longing to dump my bags and take off up that road into the quiet.

But Albert wanted to talk. More than that, he wanted a conversation. For Albert a conversation is chiefly a game of skill. Nothing raises his spirits more than a good-natured, lively jousting-match with friends. A bit of gossip, a touch of banter, together with a vigorous exchange of opinions on whatever subject comes to hand. Albert would have felt right at home in one of those eighteenth-century London coffee houses frequented by Swift or Johnson.

You can forget as he swirls about in conversation with great agility that movement of any kind these days is difficult for him. And he won't put up with what he calls '*les futilités*'—airy-fairy claptrap of any kind. He likes you to speak from your own experience, not repeat something somebody else has said or written. I'm sure I've even heard him quote Gide on the subject: 'It's not enough for me to *read* that the sands on the beach are soft, I want my bare feet to feel it.' Generally, however, he makes his point with mangoes. 'Mangoes,' he is much given to saying, once you get him started on almost any subject—Sanskrit poetry, St Augustine, Pondicherry, anything really—'have a taste that can't be imagined by anyone who hasn't eaten one.' Then, seizing the high ground, he generally goes on: 'A mango-lover can explain the taste in terms of melons or papayas, but in the end words will fail him. If you want to know what a mango tastes like, you have to taste one yourself.' What Albert means is that words will fail *you*, not him, in this discussion of things he has tasted many times. Clearly relishing the silence his mention of mangoes always produces, if only momentarily, he usually takes a sip of tea at this point (his years in Pondicherry mean that there's always a pot of it within reach) and sits back waiting for you to make the next ill-advised move. He has a softer side, but, on the whole, he likes to keep you on your toes.

So when he finally asked me, while clearing away the remains of the curried fish that first evening, what I was doing in the south of France this time, and Daniel said, a touch too quickly, that I was there to 'play hide-and-seek with André Gide', I wasn't too surprised to hear him say: 'I met him once, you know.'

'Who? Gide?'

'Yes, not long before he died.'

'Good grief! Where did you meet him?'

'In Cannes, as a matter of fact, in the foyer of the Hôtel d'Angleterre. It was my first trip to Europe. I can't have been more than eighteen.'

'How extraordinary!'

'Not really. If you stayed anywhere between Beirut and the Bay of Biscay long enough in those days, he was sure to turn up eventually.'

'Did you speak to him?' 'No, he spoke to me.'

'Perhaps he thought you were the bellboy. He often took a fancy to bellboys.'

Albert was only faintly amused. 'No, he thought I might be Tunisian.' It was true: even now, nearing eighty, there was something about Albert's skin and carriage that could have been North African. A grace. His hair was white, but his eyes were sharp and black, and you could tell straight away that as a young man loitering in the foyer of the Hôtel d'Angleterre he'd have caught Gide's eye in a flash. It all came from India, of course. He was defiantly French, but clearly out in Pondicherry the family line had become pleasingly blurred at some stage.

'What did he say?'

'Oh, I can't remember—it was over fifty years ago. Nothing terribly interesting. Famous people don't necessarily say anything interesting, you know, not even to each other.'

'He wasn't trying to pick you up or anything?'

'I'm not sure I'd have noticed, to tell you the truth.

I was from Pondicherry. Do try the Roquefort—it's very good.'

'How did he come across? Did you like him?'

'No, not at all. There was something cold about him, I thought.'

'Predatory?' (This was Daniel.)

Albert considered this word carefully as he spread a dab of quince paste onto his cheese. 'No, I wouldn't say predatory, I didn't feel that he was about to pounce... no, no, he was quite charming, as I remember, perhaps even a touch coquettish. But cold. There was something mask-like about his face. Striking, even at his age, but waxen. One can't help one's face, I know.' He considered Daniel's. 'To tell you the truth, I've never really liked Gide, neither the man nor the books. I only read him because the Vatican banned him. But that was a few years later. It was a mortal sin, you see, to read any of his works, so obviously one was obliged to have a go.'

'He's still banned, as a matter of fact,' I said, reaching for the Roquefort.

'Really? I can't say I follow the manœuvres of the Vatican with close attention. Besides, at my age, mortal sin is a very hazy concept.'

'What did you read first? No, let me guess: *Fruits of the Earth*.'

'Top marks. How did you know?'

'I think half of France read *Fruits of the Earth* in late adolescence.'

'I didn't.' (This was Daniel again.)

'Then you should, young man,' Albert said, 'it will corrupt you very nicely before it's too late. But don't delay—it soon loses its savour.' Daniel looked pleased and immediately reached for the Roquefort. 'What is it about Gide that you've never liked?' I genuinely wanted to know.

'I feel a sort of distaste for him. He makes me feel

queasy. Something about him strikes me as on the nose. And as for his books, it's odd: they're undoubtedly brilliant, especially the later ones (*The Vatican Cellars*, for instance, or *The Counterfeiters*), but they don't stay with me. Something about sexually ambiguous young men behaving badly—that's all I can recall. They never became my *friends*—do you know what I mean?—the way ... oh, I don't know ... Proust or even Turgenev or Dickens did. Elegant, but cold. The diaries, I must say, are marvellous ... at least in small doses.'

'But what makes you queasy?' This interested me.

He wasn't the only one to feel this way. 'Is it the sexual thing?'

'You mean the cruising for boys? Well, it's hardly edifying, is it? There's something sordid about it, you have to admit. Trawling the boulevards of Paris for street kids and beggars, with his wife back at home in Normandy polishing the furniture and saying her prayers; all those trips to North Africa to fumble with urchins he met up back alleys and in public gardens ... no, there's not much there to admire. There's something self-indulgent and irresponsible about it—a grown man doesn't behave like that. At my age I really don't care much any more what consenting adults do in private—but these boys were not adults.'

'Well, they weren't children, either,' I said. 'They were adolescents, they knew what he was interested in, they weren't forced to go with him—he made them an offer and they struck a bargain. And nobody ever complained about what happened, remember. Not the boys, their mothers, their fathers—nobody. Ever. Not once in sixty years. What was a homosexual supposed to do fifty or a hundred years ago? Spend his life sitting chastely at home salivating over Latin poets? What were his options? You have to take into account the times he lived in.'

Albert wasn't going to go down that track. I sometimes wondered if, despite his apparent open-mindedness, he secretly found something about homosexuals in general unpalatable, but refrained from saying so in case he gave the impression of siding with the Christian moralists. He wouldn't have gone so far as to claim that homosexuality was the result of epilepsy, the influence of Uranus or the westward spread of the Bulgarians, as his schoolteacher friend from the walking group, Monsieur Gilbert, did, but I had the feeling he found it at the very least uncalled-for and believed that it was getting worse. 'Be that as it may,' he said, 'something about the way he treated his wife was on the nose. It was a *mariage blanc*, you know. No sex at all. Not even once.'

Of course I knew. Everyone knew, except possibly Daniel, who perked up considerably at this intriguing snippet of information. 'So why did he get married?'

'Because he loved her.' I knew that was a fairly meaningless thing to say, but it was also true. 'From the age of about thirteen, as a matter of fact.'

'Like a sister, do you mean?'

'Well, I don't have a sister,' I said, 'so I'm no expert, but no, not like a sister. Obsessively, totally, the way people love Jesus.'

'Spiritually, do you mean?' Daniel was goading me. He knew I regarded that word with suspicion.

'If you like.'

There it was again: that inexplicably intense desire in me to defend this man I'd never known personally from a sweeping dismissal of his way of life, of living out who he was in those utterly different times. It made me snappish. From what I'd heard, there was something pretty 'on the nose' about the way Albert had treated his *own* two wives, if it came to that. Or was it three? (The walking group was a hotbed of delectable gossip about all the members' marital arrangements, but the details could never be relied upon.) However, I said nothing. Daniel was as tense as a cat watching a mousehole.

'So . . . did he "trawl the boulevards" all his life?' 'He enjoyed the odd casual encounter until he was almost eighty. And not just on the boulevards.' '*Eighty!*' I could tell from the expression on his face that Daniel found the very idea of an eighty-year-old man having sexual adventures not just mind-boggling, but faintly disgusting.

'Being old doesn't mean you have no appetite, young man,' Albert said sharply, 'although the opportunity to satisfy it certainly gets rarer with the passing years.' We all sat for a while in silence, the air heavy with what each of us was leaving unsaid. 'I know what it is,' Albert said all of a sudden, 'I know what I find so off-putting about André Gide. You reminded me of it, Daniel, when you mentioned playing hide-and-seek. One of his friends—Roger Martin du Gard I think it was, another fine writer whose books leave no impression on me, very close they were ... nothing *irregular*, I'm sure ... in those days friends could get close without anyone getting jittery about it. Anyway, he said that Gide was continually playing hide-and-seek with *himself*. That's it exactly. *With himself.* Everyone else, including his wife, just had to sit back and watch the show. Now you see me, now you don't. I don't like that. What that woman must have gone through!' We all sat for a moment, pretending to be imagining Madeleine's plight.

'I think that what you can't forgive him is that he didn't suffer,' I said. 'Wasn't punished, wasn't remorseful and didn't ask for forgiveness. Wasn't *pitiable*. He found a way to have his cake and eat it too. He got off scot-free. So you turn away with distaste.'

'He got off scot-free because he was rich, not because he'd found the key to happiness. Besides, his happiness, if that's what it was, made plenty of other people unhappy.'

'Who, for instance?' 'Madeleine for a start.'

'Madeleine was *born* miserable.' It wasn't really quite what I believed, but this was a conversation, not a seminar. Still, when her husband once asked her if she'd ever been happy, her cheerless reply was: 'There have been a few oases.' Albert was about to hit back—this is what he enjoyed: a bit of thrust and parry—when the kettle in the kitchen started whistling and he hobbled off to make some tea. 'She didn't *want* sex with him,' I called after him, although I was hardly in any position to know what she'd wanted. 'From the moment her mother ran off with her lover—how old was Madeleine at the time? Fifteen?—she spent the rest of her life redeeming her mother's sin. Her coin was chastity. She might have liked to have children, but I suspect she'd have preferred to have them by immaculate conception.' Silence in the kitchen. When he came back in with the tea, I could see that for the moment the subject was closed.

Madeleine, Madeleine. As if Albert gave a fig for the sufferings of Madeleine Gide. What really rankled with Albert, I was sure of it, is that Gide was perfectly happy without playing by Albert's rules for happiness. As Gide expressed it in his diary, for believers, whatever you achieve without saying your beads doesn't count. Religion is mostly a form of banking, after all—'the best-trained soul is the one that best keeps its accounts', as Julius de Baraglioul explains to his brother-in-law in *The Vatican Cellars*—and as far as Albert was concerned Gide was fiddling the books.

Over in a corner beside the vast stone fireplace

amongst various gew-gaws from Pondicherry, my eye came to rest on the black-and-white photograph of Albert's Living Goddess. There was a tiny oil-lamp burning in front of it in the half-dark. Ma Somebody-or-other. She was smiling at us serenely with just a touch of sultriness. She lived in Pondicherry. Sooner or later the conversation would be skewed in the direction of the image in the lamplight—it always was. In the deepening silence I could feel the moment ripening. I yawned and said I might take myself off to bed.

Albert's eyes lit up. He'd very much taken to Daniel, I suspected, despite his youth. Daniel gave the impression of having tried quite a few mangoes on his trips to India, and there was something about him that obviously made Albert think he could be tempted to try a few more. Even as I bade them goodnight and set off for the guest room in the barn, I could tell that Albert was planning his next move. I was a lost cause as far as Ma Whatshername was concerned, but this interesting young man with the shaven head I'd brought with me was another matter entirely. Albert pretended to be clearing the table while listening to Daniel idly picking out a tune or two on the piano by the window, but I knew that he'd soon begin carefully laying a little velvet trap for him to step into. The bait would be that Living Goddess of his over in the corner. Daniel would walk right into it. They'd be there half the night. *Sauve qui peut.* I was off.

◆

By the next morning it was clear that I had been upstaged. Whatever had transpired after I'd gone to bed, Albert and (I had no doubt) his Living Goddess gave every appearance of having captivated Daniel completely. On his bedside table when I awoke lay some esoteric text with a cover illustration of a blue-faced god playing a flute, entwined with a smiling goddess. They seemed to have far too many arms between them. Of *Fruits of the Earth*, which I had half-hoped Albert might lend him, there was no sign. By the time I came out into the garden, Albert and Daniel were already enjoying breakfast in the dappled shade of the nettletree on the terrace above the stream. Albert was regaling him with stories of old Pondy, which Daniel was now clearly very interested in visiting next time he was in India. However, when the conversation veered away from French colonial architecture and the jade-green sea towards ashrams and Sri Aurobindo, I could see us sitting there talking about the Chain of Ignorance and the infinite manifestations of Vishnu until nightfall, so I suggested an excursion.

'How about the Popes' Palace in Avignon? Have you ever been to Avignon, Daniel?' He hadn't, but seemed unenthusiastic. Perhaps the Popes' Palace had been the wrong place to start, under the circumstances. 'What about Nîmes, then? There's the Roman amphitheatre . . .

What else is there in Nîmes, Albert?'

'Well, there are a couple of museums . . . More tea, anyone?'

There was always the old abbey of St Guilhem-le Désert not far away in the mountains; it even boasts a few real Benedictine monks and a splinter of the True Cross. And there was the Roman aqueduct at Pont-du-Gard as well, a tourist cliché but undeniably impressive. However, Daniel didn't look as if he was in a hurry to go anywhere. He seemed to be floating. To be honest, I didn't particularly want to go sightseeing myself, it was just a hook to hang an outing on. You can't just motor about. We sipped our tea in silence.

'So tell me more about this Sri Aurobindo,' Daniel said eventually, coming down to earth. 'What's his line?'

'Ah, well, you see, for Sri Aurobindo, the Brahman is attained through a particular kind of yoga called *purna-yoga*, which is . . .'

'I might leave you to it,' I said. 'Go for a walk up the river.'

'Good idea,' Albert said. 'Such a beautiful morning. Take an apple with you.'

Then *pop*! I froze. *Pop! Pop! Pop!* Hunters. Up in the forest. It made my flesh crawl.

'Oh, I forgot,' Albert said apologetically, 'the hunters are out today. Not the best day for a walk up the river.'

Twice a week hunters in red caps jump into their vans and head for the forest around Tornac to kill things—wild boar mostly, sometimes each other. They even prowl through the vineyards slaughtering hares and pheasants. You see their white vans of death parked by the roadside wherever you go on those days, each waiting for its load of carcasses.

'Come on, let's go for a drive, Daniel,' I said. 'I don't want to spend the day listening to . . . *that*.' More bursts of gunfire from the hills behind us. Not loud, almost like children's firecrackers. *Pop! Pop!* Silence. *Pop! Pop! Pop!* 'Let's go into Anduze, get the papers, browse around . . . I don't know, we could go up to the castle if you like and have a poke about—you like ruins.' Daniel was being particularly kite-like that morning, bobbing about above us, as it were, just out of reach. He needed to be firmly reeled in. 'So how about it?'

'*OK*,' he said in French, '*pourquoi pas?*' And with one of those ambiguous smiles he'd picked up in Sikkim or Ladakh, he pushed back his chair. (In a certain mood, usually first thing in the morning and late at night, Daniel can be surprisingly accommodating.) 'Meet you at the car.'

♦

'What did you mean last night by "playing hide-and-seek with André Gide"?' I said, once we'd crossed the stream and begun to thread our way towards Anduze amongst the vineyards. I said it partly to break the silence, but partly, too, because it was such an odd thing to say.

'Well, that's what you seem to be doing. He hides away in Normandy or down here in Uzès—or in one of his books—and you run around trying to ferret him out. You'll be off to Tunisia next, or was it Algeria?'

'Both.' I could see what Daniel meant, but that wasn't quite it. I thought of something one of his biographers had said: Gide tended to appear and disappear like the Cheshire Cat, leaving just a grin. There was a pause while Daniel felt around in the glove box amongst the maps and condoms for a piece of chocolate, trying at the same time not to swerve off the narrow road into a vineyard.

'And I also get the feeling that you half expect *him* to come looking for *you*.' 'What does *that* mean?'

'I get the feeling that you'd somehow like him to seek you out and recognise you—throw open a cupboard door and catch you hiding there in the dark. Naked.' Naked? Why naked? 'And then call you by name and lead you out into the light. Want some chocolate?' I took two pieces.

I knew that Daniel thought there was something a bit bizarre, even unsavoury, about my feelings for Gide—my '*sympathie*', as he put it in French—but this put a different cast on it. He kept calling him my '*âme sœur*'— literally my 'sister soul', but for some reason the way he said it made it sound vaguely indecent. For Daniel, Gide was someone you read at school, and, like any normal schoolboy, he'd found books like *La Symphonie pastorale* (a Swiss pastor's diary—sex and religion in a joyless Swiss village) unutterably dreary, although it's unaccountably popular with the Japanese, I've heard. Apart from that, and the fact that he'd won the Nobel Prize and was long dead, all he seemed to know about him was that he'd been a 'pederast'. Something about this seemed to irk him.

'He wasn't a *paedophile*, you know,' I'd said to him when the subject had first come up back in Paris, 'if that's what's bothering you. He didn't fiddle with little boys. He was a *pederast*.'

'No, that's not what bothers me. Why would I care if he was a pederast? What *is* a pederast, anyway, I mean, technically speaking?'

The French are oddly sloppy in their use of this word. You can be fixated on the over eighty and still get called a 'pederast'.

'Oh, in his case, it means he definitely liked them ... how did he put it? ... in the flower of their youth. The first flowering, admittedly, nothing too bushy, but still—youths. On second thoughts, that's not what *he* said, it's what somebody else said.'

'I see. How Greek.'

'Exactly.'

'Ephebes.'

I smiled. 'That's the word. He liked them at the age

when a child is no longer a child, between puberty and joining the army.'

'Jail bait nowadays, all the same.'

'Sometimes, in some places.'

'Does it bother *you*, this pederasty thing?'

'A bit, I suppose ... I can't quite make up my mind. His idea of a good time was hardly the depths of depravity, though: it was basically a few bouts of mutual pleasuring. *Complicité dans l'onanisme.* Do you like that phrase?'

'You mean they jerked each other off.'

'He always put it more poetically, but yes. Caressing, he called it. You'd have been bored witless. All rather juvenile, really. No wonder he felt "rejuvenated" by it. Still, anything predatory bothers me.'

'Was your Gide predatory?'

'He did go out on the prowl ... but then so do you. Are you predatory?'

He'd smiled, a sliver of chocolate stuck to one lip. 'You make me sound like a panther,' he said.

What could I say?

Now, trundling towards Anduze past all those sprawling industrial outlets and showrooms—pottery, furniture, automobiles—that seem to dot the countryside around French towns, this conversation came back to me. I even remembered the truck we'd been stuck behind at the time. j. sienkiewicz warszawa, said the sign on the back. I remembered every letter.

'Something about Gide seems to annoy you,' I said.

'I really don't know much about him.'

Few do any more, it seems, even in France. What *I* remember about Gide is not his devilishly clever novels. (He claimed they weren't novels at all, but *'soties'*, a kind of Early-Renaissance satirical farce. If he'd been English, he'd probably have written 'nonsense literature', like Lewis Carroll or Edward Lear. *Tristram Shandy* also springs to mind. The English don't discharge their panic over the meaningless of life or God's non-existence by being clever, but by being stupendously silly.) What I remember about Gide is the junctures in our two lives at which we seem to have chosen similar paths—left here, right there ... goodness me, is that *you* again, Monsieur Gide, we seem to bump into each other wherever we go. Sometimes it feels as if I'm shadowing him, while pretending I'm not. Now and again it really does feel as if he's shadowing me. To put it more accurately, it sometimes feels as if he's my invisible opponent in a game of chess, taking pleasure less in the game (at which he's a much more skilful player than I am) than in watching my reactions to his moves.

Needless to say, I wasn't born into the French upper middle-class, but I was, like him, an only child, haunted by exciting fantasies of other boys' bodies. (I didn't, however, masturbate in class or under the dining-room table with the boy from next door.) And at the same time, unfazed by the paradox, I thrilled, like the adolescent André, to the stories spiralling out of the New Testament, and especially to the hunt for new meanings for these stories, radically spiritual meanings hidden under the dross of doctrine. The older I get, the more I think these two radically different passions are two sides of the same coin. Or perhaps they are more like the biblical tares and wheat. Jesus' parable advises us to let the weeds and the wheat grow side by side until the harvest, when the weeds can be gathered up and burnt, 'lest while ye gather up the tares, ye root up the wheat also with them'. They are nourished by the same soil: in my case, a lust for intimacy, for rawness, for nakedness in another's presence, ideally God's, but in the meantime the postman or even the little girl next door will do. It's very confusing.

Although we were both bookish and in love with language, the young André had a much finer education than I had: I was not the son of a professor of Roman law and a mother with a castle in Normandy. In our suburban bungalow my father did not read to me from the Old Testament or Homer, let alone *A Thousand and One Nights*: he read the newspaper, listened to the radio and took me to the library to borrow whatever I wanted—children's adventure stories, mostly, as well as anything I could get my hands on about Iceland. All the same, there are parallels. Swimming alone upstream, as we both knew we would be all our lives, we adopted surprisingly similar manœuvres to save ourselves from drowning: we both went to North Africa in our early twenties to forget who we were supposed to be; and we both felt a deep and complicated passion for Russia and the Russians, although Gide didn't go there until he was in his mid-sixties, whereas I went there to study as a young man. Russia for both of us was an amplification of who we would like to be, not a forgetting. We both married soon after our mothers' deaths as a way of holding onto our essential goodness and loved our wives in a way we couldn't find the right word for; we both gave ourselves over to literature at a time when there was diminishing confidence in the point of telling conventional stories, both of us constitutionally unable to tell stories with well-mannered storylines, not having anything of immediate consequence to say, although we did know how to pleasingly arrange our inconsequentialities; we both drifted while still young into the guiltless enjoyment of a wide variety of emotional and sexual entanglements with our own sex, some lasting ten minutes, others a lifetime; and we both found our Bibles not so much forgotten as lost amongst the piles of other bibles littering our mental libraries. And he was a passionate traveller, as I am, although I'm not sure that I only travel to places where there's a chance of fornication, as he said he did. I would put it more delicately: I like to go to places where there are possibilities for eros. In short, we both moved around the world with a strange kind of combative dreaminess, if that makes sense. He died when I was seven years old, having just won the Nobel Prize for Literature, acknowledged as one of the twentieth century's greatest writers and thinkers. There is no real connection between us, even as a teenager his mental universe was infinitely broader than mine is now, and he had a moral courage, an openness about who he was and what he believed, that I in my suburban way could never emulate. I know all that, and yet I want to draw close to him, to understand him better, to protest my friendship for him, to watch him from the wings. If that's what 'playing hide-and-seek' with André Gide means, then I'm guilty.

Before I could say any of this to Daniel, though, we'd parked the car in a side street in Anduze. It's a rather higgledy-piggledy town on the banks of the Gard, with a main square bustling with Dutch holidaymakers in shorts. We headed towards the market strung out along some of the ancient alleyways on the hill behind the main square. Scarves, belts, earrings, T-shirts, pottery, honey, endives, spices, bottles of wine, second-hand books—all the usual bric-à-brac and local produce under striped umbrellas, very gay. Daniel's eyes lit up. He rarely buys anything, but likes to finger things and engage in a bit of banter with the stallholders. He thinks it puts him in touch with the *real* France. This wasn't the moment for a welter of abstract nouns. With a grin he vanished into the throng.

4.

ANDUZE

How on earth we ended up at the Musée du Désert on the other side of Anduze that morning is a mystery. Perhaps we'd seen it signposted and, misunderstanding the word '*désert*', I'd talked Daniel into taking us there, expecting Tuaregs and maps of ancient trade routes across the Sahara. So when the severe-looking woman behind the desk fixed me with a not unfriendly but dispassionate stare as we came in and asked: '*Vous êtes protestant, monsieur?*' I was rather taken aback. 'If you are,' she went on, her close-cropped silver hair glistening in the sunlight, 'we can probably tell you if any of your forebears were sent to the galleys, imprisoned, deported, hanged ... we have excellent records.' What sort of museum *was* this?

Daniel, who was browsing amongst the books and

pamphlets on sale near the door, enjoying some of the lurid illustrations, turned when he heard the question and quizzically raised one eyebrow. What was I going to say? He was waiting.

'Well, yes I am,' I said, 'but not from these parts.' 'I am, too,' said Daniel, walking over to the desk, his lips parted in one of his irresistible grins—he has very fine teeth. 'From a very long line.' The truth was that he came from a long line of pious Catholics, although one eccentric uncle of his did claim to be a Cathar—the last. Not surprisingly, no amount of scouring of the records produced any forebears who had been martyrs. Daniel put on his philosophical look.

The museum has nothing to do with deserts, as I should have known, at least not in the Saharan sense. '*Désert*' refers to the wilderness in which the local Protestants were forced to live and worship—those, at least, who didn't escape abroad or weren't slaughtered—when the Catholic Church unleashed its reign of terror against them in the late seventeenth century. A rambling maze of poky rooms and passageways—almost a hamlet in its own right—the museum occupies the house of a famous eighteenth-century Protestant rebel and pig farmer in the forested hills just outside Anduze. To this day, on the first Sunday in September each year, thousands of Protestants from all over France gather here beneath the oaks and chestnuts in remembrance of the clandestine assemblies that took place in barns and forest glades in these parts during the years of persecution. If you were caught worshipping at one of these assemblies at the height of the terror, you could be hanged or shot on the spot. Tornac had been a particular hotbed of Protestant revolt, it turned out, and a lot of fighting had taken place in the forests around Albert's house in the early eighteenth century. Quite a few of its residents were condemned to the galleys for life.

After spending an hour or two wandering from room to room past displays of miniature Bibles, mobile pulpits, savage edicts and paintings of the faithful rowing the galleys with Turks, being tortured and assembling for worship in the wilderness—all the paraphernalia of French Protestantism—I began to understand what 'being Protestant' meant in these surroundings. Madame had not been asking me whether I was a Lutheran or believed in transubstantiation, but, taking me for a Frenchman, what sort of Frenchman I was.

On the way out Daniel purchased a booklet on heresy in the Middle Ages. Then, in a small café tucked in behind one of the museum's rose-covered walls, we found a sunny spot to sit and mull over what we'd just seen. It was still quite early, so there was nobody much about.

'You should've told her you were interested in André Gide,' Daniel said, after flicking through his book on heresy in silence for a few moments. I'd been contemplating the explosion of white roses climbing up the wall across the laneway: they were soothing after the horrors inside. 'That would've got her on side.'

'Oh, I don't think so. Gide wasn't the kind of Protestant she'd be likely to approve of.'

'He was one of the best-known Protestants in the country. Even I knew he was one.'

'Yes, well, that wasn't the only thing he was famous for. Why did you tell her you were a Protestant? That was cheeky.'

Daniel ran a hand across his gleaming shaved skull. 'Why not? She was pleased. Anyway, perhaps I am, in my fashion. *Je proteste*.'

What was this now? I felt vaguely irritated. 'No, you're not. You don't even believe in God.' Neither, for that matter, do many Protestants these days, but I was on a roll. 'You believe in a whole throng of . . . whatever you call them. Demigods. Bodhisattvas.'

'Bodhisattvas are quite different.' He just smiled and stretched like a cat.

'You've got an elephant god beside your bed. You . . . *chant* and so on. All those giggling gurus of yours—Sri this, Sri that. That's got nothing to do with being a Protestant.'

'Well, I'm not a Catholic, that's a start.'

'That's not the point.'

'So what is the point, exactly?'

The point, as far as I was concerned at that moment, was that the memories we'd just seen brought to life so vividly in the museum were not his (or mine, I have to admit), as they were Gide's, for instance. Gide's roots on his father's side of the family were planted right here in Languedoc where these massacres and persecutions had taken place. His grandfather Tancrède was already an adolescent when the last mass murders of Protestants took place at Uzès during the so-called White Terror. As a Frenchman Daniel had no right to be cavalier about these memories.

'Even if your ancestors *had* been Huguenots,' I went on, 'which they weren't, even if your great-great-great-grandfather had been strung up on that oak tree right over there for listening to a sermon, you still wouldn't be a Protestant. You don't *think* like a Protestant.'

'What's it to you?' He was still smiling, but his smile had a slightly different edge to it. 'Why does it matter to you how I think? You take it all too seriously.' Why did it? And was Daniel being attractively serene or maddeningly indifferent to what I felt?

It has always mattered to me where people stand on these questions. The orientation of the soul (the psyche, the self we think we love)—and that's what it amounts to—matters, and in a friend it matters deeply. Maybe Wilde was right and there *is* no soul or psyche or self, just layers of masks, or maybe we truly are just orchestras of neurones without a conductor, as so many scientists believe, but it feels as if there's a self there and loving someone is hard to do unless you think there is and like its colouring.

It's important to me that the people I'm close to should have thought these things through. At some level it has always bothered me—even as a child it bothered me—when people just say this or that is what they believe and then fall silent. Or that it's all nonsense, all that business about God and miracles and heaven and hell, and then stare off into space—or watch football or go shopping—as if that settles that. Obviously nobody we might know *believes* any of it (unless they're American)—sky-gods, the afterlife, the virgin birth, the resurrection, and so on—although some may have *faith* in it. They may be able to imagine it, for example, and hope it's true, they may have contrived to suspend their disbelief in it, but they can't possibly positively believe it, not even the Pope can in truth *believe* it, it's obviously all nonsense—gorgeous, perfumed, symphonic, zany nonsense, but nonsense. I doubt it was ever even meant to be *believed* in the way we might believe that Marco Polo went to China, say (for which there's also scant evidence). That doesn't mean we should stop talking about what's behind these stories, though. We must keep talking about what's behind them, especially with our friends, otherwise . . . Otherwise what? Otherwise the banality of our lives would become too obvious to bear. I had a stab at explaining some of this to Daniel, but I could tell I wasn't getting far.

'I think you might've read too much Dostoyevsky as a boy,' Daniel said eventually, trying to make me lighten up. 'People have believed in star signs for thousands of years as well, and you think that's all nonsense, too. Should we also keep talking about the horoscope? Or what about elves? Should we keep discussing elves?'

'Oh, shut up.'

'What star sign *are* you, by the way?'

I'd have liked to hit him, but that could wait. Anyway, he was probably right about Dostoyevsky. Dostoyevsky, Gogol, Tolstoy—they'd all been godbotherers and I'd no doubt spent far too much of my youth taking them all too seriously, not to mention more arcane thinkers. I caught sight of the waiter bringing our coffees and apple turnovers and brightened.

'For whatever reason, these things are important to me, I can't help it,' I said, as the waiter ambled closer. There was something about his crooked nose, I noticed, which was curiously attractive.

'But why?'

'Because ... oh, I don't know ...' Easier just to enjoy the coffee and *chaussons aux pommes*.

'Yes, you do.'

'Because there's no reason at all to think that *this*'—and here I flung one hand out almost sending the waiter's tray flying—'is the only reality. Why should it be?'

'No reason at all.'

'So I like to be with people who are throwing open all the windows and doors and looking to see what else might be out there. I just can't believe that it's Mary

Mother of God and a bunch of angels. Or Bodhisattvas. But more than that, there's something completely *intolerable* about life if this is all there is, this painful messiness. From my point of view, at any rate. Completely intolerable. If it makes no more sense than a record played backwards, it's hardly worth the struggle.' I paused, thinking he might ask me what I thought was 'completely intolerable' about life—it was such a school-masterly word and, whatever predicaments I might get myself into from time to time, I was not dying of malaria in an African refugee camp, for instance—but he didn't. He looked down at his hands. I think he knew. 'So we have to keep talking about these things. At the very least we have to talk to each other about how to reconcile ourselves to what's intolerable.'

'Not about how to transcend it?' He was still looking down.

I was torn. Naturally I'd like to 'transcend' death and suffering, who wouldn't? But there was something about that slippery word on Daniel's lips that put me on my guard. I didn't want this conversation to turn Himalayan. 'All I'm saying is that this is how we've talked about dealing with the unacceptable side to being human since time began and it's too soon to stop.'

'We *can* stop asking the same old questions, though, and getting the same old answers.' The sun was glinting on his shaved head, lending him that slightly monkish look I rather like. I like it because there is actually nothing monkish about him at all. 'Anyway, I thought you once said you went to Morocco when you were young to forget precisely all these things—religion and so on. Forget who you were, stop leading a double life. Just like André Gide. So . . . ?' Now he was being mischievous. He'd only mentioned Gide to needle me. But he was quite right about remembering and forgetting: I had indeed gone to Morocco at twenty-two precisely to forget what I was now saying should not be forgotten, as had Gide to Tunisia and Algeria. For the first time in his young life he carefully left his Bible at home when he left for North Africa, and, although I took mine with me, I didn't open it. It didn't work for either of us. We couldn't forget. It didn't work because there are surely two kinds of forgetting: one is forever and the other is a momentary frenzy. Well, the frenzy might last a month or even a few years, but it doesn't blot out memory for good. It's just taking your hidden self out for an airing.

'Even some Buddhist monks,' I said to Daniel, as we walked back to the car, 'have days of divine madness. It keeps them sane. They take up with loose women and go on drunken rampages.' I would have waved goodbye to Crooked Nose, but he wasn't looking.

'Yes, it's called "Crazy Wisdom". It's Tibetan.' How annoying that he should know that. 'And it's not about "keeping sane", it's about flux. It's about taming instead of clinging, and then letting go. I have the feeling that your Gide may have been too Protestant to believe in flux. He probably believed in virtue and sin.' I think he partly meant me. But he had a point: Protestants are particularly given to dualities such as sin and virtue, belief and unbelief, spirit and matter. It's one thing or the other with us. Catholics, on the other hand, have ways of striking a bargain with God. Flux is something they understand.

'Whatever,' I said in English. 'Anyway, I think that that's the kind of forgetting I wanted to do in Morocco. I wanted a burst of "Crazy Wisdom".'

We drove in silence through the woods above the river, heading down towards the plain and Tornac. At times there was something *stilled* about Daniel which I found both frustrating and deeply attractive. You could drown in it. It wasn't until we'd come out the other side of Anduze that the silence was broken.

'Anyway,' he said, 'in what way are *you* Protestant?'

'To tell you the truth, it's something I've only recently become aware of.'

'I mean, do you believe in the Trinity and accept Jesus as your Saviour?'

'Certainly not. Do I look like someone who believes in the Trinity? There's nothing about a trinity in the Bible.' I wished I hadn't said that, I'd laid a trap for myself, but I had. 'But to explain I'd have to tell you about something that happened a few weeks ago in Portugal.'

'Portugal? That seems an unlikely place.'

'In Oporto. I had a small epiphany in Oporto.'

'How intriguing. I wouldn't have thought you were the type.'

'Then I'll tell you.' And, as the vineyards and old stone villages outside Anduze drifted past, I told him about my illuminating moment in the cathedral in Oporto. It wasn't exactly a psychic volte-face, and it didn't take me straight to Algiers, but, as if foreshadowing my encounter with the caterpillar in Normandy soon afterwards, it did stir the embers of my dormant kinship with André Gide. It was another thing I could never discuss with Yacoub, although Daniel, in his fashion, might be more sympathetic.

The Small Epiphany In Oporto

What brought it on is hard to say. There was no organ playing that morning in the cathedral (and I am susceptible to organs in vaulted spaces), and I don't remember feeling particularly *transparent* either, as I do sometimes when a bolt of perception is about to hit. On the contrary, I was feeling rather cluttered, Oporto being a raucous, cluttered, cluttering sort of city.

It had nothing to do with spiritual force-lines, either—unlike Albert, I have no time at all for feng shui. All the same, the cathedral in Oporto is sublimely situated on a crag above the old red-roofed quarter of the city, which topples and slides down the hill in a maze of crooked, scabby lanes to the river. Up here flying buttresses and soaring towers with cupolas; down there tumult, crumbling tenements and then water; up here silence and a rose window glowing like the eye of heaven itself; down there bustling squalor, cats fighting, roosters crowing, women screeching, fish frying—and then the water. Right in front of the cathedral, across a stone archway leading down into the slum, someone had scrawled in black paint: *bem-vindo a inferno* (welcome to hell).

Wherever I see it, something about this arrangement—the citadel with its crumpled skirts of roofs and laneways falling away below it, and then the water—always hits me like the echo of an inner landscape. Like a tuning fork, I begin to sing the same note as what I'm seeing. I first noticed it at the Parthenon in Athens when I was twenty-one.

Entering the cathedral in a state of mild curiosity, I felt at first as if I'd wandered into a Hindu temple doubling as a railway station. Crowds of Belgians and Germans were wandering about its stony vastness with backpacks and bags of shopping, staring at the idols, the paintings, the altars and each other. There was a low hum of conversation echoing around the nave. Cameras flashed. A tent-shaped Englishwoman slapped her whining daughter.

A graça de Nosso Senhor Jesus Cristo . . . At the far end of the nave, I became aware of a robed figure softly intoning something into a microphone. He was flanked by six women, no longer young, listening to him in reverential silence. Nobody else at all in that whole vast edifice seemed even to have noticed he was there. Slipping into a seat in the front row, I tried to cut myself off from the hubbub all around me for a moment or two and let the music of the priest's words wash over me. *Deus Todo-Poderoso ... os nossos pecados e nos conduza à vida eterna* ... I really couldn't understand much that this man in gold-threaded vestments was saying, something consoling about Jesus and God omnipotent, but it hardly mattered. He kept speaking softly into the void, joined in murmured responses from his six parishioners. *Glória a Vós, Senhor. Glória ... Glória ...* I looped in and out of his golden *glórias*. He was gold, the chancel behind him was a wildly soaring, baroque extravaganza in gold. *Creio no Espírito Santo ... Creio na Igreja una, santa, católica e apostólica ...* The six old ladies and I sat floating on the sound of his gold-encrusted voice.

But now there seemed to be a strange gulf opening up between us. And it seemed to be growing wider before my eyes. *Hossana nas alturas ...* I had the bizarre feeling that they were floating away from me into the apse, leaving me behind in the nave. And not just away from me, but up. They were being gathered up. And then it struck me: every last loose thread of these six women's lives had already been lovingly gathered up and woven into the sacred tapestry of the Church. Their lives had been *redeemed*, not by understanding, not by seeing Truth face to face, but by being gathered up into the Church.

For me, left stranded in my anorak in the front pew, there was no sacred tapestry to weave myself into, 'sacred' being a word I had long since emptied of any meaning. No church, however universal, no priest, however gorgeously robed, no altar, even if carved from solid gold, no chalice, no bread or wine, no incantations, no relics, no temples or groves or stones, or anything else in the universe to me was 'sacred'.

Hossana nas alturas... Their cries of joy were growing slowly fainter as they receded from me with gathering speed. I felt a stab of anguish—no, not anguish exactly, but a pang of sorrow—at the growing gulf between us. They had found a way to redeem what I never could: the utter ordinariness of everyday existence. It's unlikely that they had much in their lives to be contrite about—and, in any case, outright wickedness is never much of a problem. It's what Dostoyevsky calls the 'lukewarm' life that it's difficult for people like me to rescue, all the bits that, in a novel, would be edited out. Last Tuesday afternoon, the whole of October, in fact entire years frittered away on forgotten conversations, tidying up the living room, reading the newspaper, cooking soup, waiting for a bus. Even if they were society matrons or countesses (which seemed unlikely since they were plainly, almost drably, dressed) these six parishioners must still have Tuesday afternoons, Octobers, even whole years like mine.

A few Bonnard canvases drifted through my mind. *O pecado do mundo,* the sin of the world ... *o pecado do mundo... o pecado do mundo...* Bonnard's paintings are sinless, just bowls of fruit, the corner of a table, a cat or two, his wife in the bath, a woman bending over in the garden... yet they are beautiful. Beauty and tradition redeem the everydayness of the lives he captures. No need of a church.

O amor de Cristo nos uniu... Now I could hardly hear them at all... *Amen!... Amen!... Amen!* And they shrank to nothing.

When I came to my senses, for the first time in my life I thought to myself: I'm a Protestant. With the church bells angrily calling after me, I strode out of the cathedral and down into the Catholic morass of Oporto towards the river.

◆

Obviously I was not a Protestant in the sense of believing that Jesus was my Saviour or that the Bible was the word of God—not, at least, by the time I got to Oporto. Obviously I didn't sing in a gospel choir or speak in tongues. I didn't even worship; the very idea of worshipping a god has always struck me as primitive. What sort of god demands to be worshipped? And just as obviously I had never been a Catholic. None of the boys at school, none of the neighbours we mixed with and none of my parents' friends was *Catholic*. That was unthinkable. 'Catholic' was something mothers of six in distant, flatter suburbs called themselves or villagers in the more primitive parts of Europe. And very picturesque it could be, too, what with all their dressing-up, processions and visions of the Virgin Mary. One bought postcards of their sacred sites while touring Italy, just as one might buy postcards of the pyramids in Egypt. Where we lived, however, in the northern suburbs of Sydney, being Catholic was barely respectable. It brought to mind men who bet on the horses and women called Carmel who smoked and wore too much lipstick. But not being Catholic didn't mean you felt Protestant. We were just us.

At the top of the hill near our house was a Catholic church that I walked past almost every day of my life, so clearly there were Catholics dotted about even amongst us. Indeed, for years I went to the nearby convent every week with my dog to learn the piano from Sister Mary Francis. Playing the piano is still inseparable in my mind from the Sacred Heart of Jesus which, unsettlingly, hung directly in front of me above the piano. I always felt it didn't like me. But Sister Mary Francis wasn't a normal person like my mother or the mother of my friends next door—she was swathed in black, had no children and wore a wimple. She could have been a priestess from some lost tribe in the Andes, as far as I was concerned, she scarcely belonged to my world at all. My dog, strange to relate, felt very much at home in the piano room at the convent with Sister Mary Francis and eventually took to spending most of his time there.

But what am I saying? My own father Tom was a long-lapsed Catholic, furnishing me with countless Catholic cousins. At a very early age, though, I sensed that they belonged to an alien clan with outlandish rituals—queer incantations, pieties and rules of their own. More tellingly, they also seemed to rest in the *bosom* of something, which we certainly did not. Nor did we wish to. Comfort was not our aim. (Gide once said he had a 'horror' of comfort and that that was his most Protestant trait.) My cousins, though, were forever echoing Sebastian in *Brideshead Revisited* who said: 'Oh dear, it's very difficult being a Catholic.' Well, it didn't look difficult at all to me. It looked complicated (this was a venial sin whereas that was a mortal sin and so on) but not *difficult*: you negotiated and bought back your innocence. Easy. We, on the other hand, had to be good. We had no horror of comfort, by the way, but we did have—and I think this *is* a very Protestant trait—a love of what I might call 'sufficiency'. Just as God's word had no need of orchestration to lead us to the light—His word was sufficient—so in our lives there was a leaning towards sufficiency rather than extravagance or lavish comfort. One aimed not to *be* poor, but to be poor in one's *needs*. You can be poor in your needs in a penthouse on Fifth Avenue. Outsiders misconstrue this respect for sufficiency as austerity—Isaiah Berlin once called pietism 'a very grand form of sour grapes': if you can't have rank and riches, you may as well settle for God—but that's to miss the point. It's more than an aesthetic, too: it's an ethic, a spiritual economy. And it wasn't joyless. The Swiss village in Gide's *Symphonie pastorale* may have been, but our lives weren't gloomy at all.

None of this meant that we thought of ourselves as Protestant, however. We were simply normal. Being what we were was the default position for any reasonable human being.

My father Tom's inclinations by the time I came along were more theosophical than anything else, but theosophy, of course, isn't a bosom. Nor was the Presbyterian Church of my mother, Jean. God might have a bosom to nestle in, if you're in a childish mood, but His is the only one available to a Presbyterian. There is no Mother Church, no Superego giving orders apart from God. It's just Him and you. And He has spoken. To each of us, personally. In the pages of the blue-covered Bible I read daily, he had not just spoken, but held forth. For the first half of my life I could hear a sort of constant haranguing in the background, like wind in the chimney or neighbours fighting. (It's astonishing how Islamic it all sounds now—God, His prophet, His book and me.) Like the adolescent Gide, I spent a lot of time when I was a teenager—and older—reading the Scriptures, especially the New Testament, instead of playing football and torturing small animals like normal boys. Just gorgeous gobbledygook to some, I know, a radiant jumble of myth and legend, but to me at the time it read more like a collection of coded messages. You could go adventuring in the Bible, misreading the map and following false trails, then getting the wind of something, something real and breathtakingly beautiful, and off you'd go haring after it, trying to pinpoint it and see it face to face. The Bible was a forest of magic words and buried somewhere underneath all those threats and prohibitions, all the exhortations and visions of pure being, I was convinced there was a truth to be unearthed, an absolute truth beyond time and space. A guide or leader could come in handy, but only insofar as he (or she, more promisingly) followed the Truth. If you had the key to the code, and didn't stray from the path, you could find it. It was somewhere there in the text. Text, not ritual. To this day even the ritual of birthday parties makes me feel as if I'm wasting my time.

Then, as the years passed, I discovered, as Protestants do, other coded texts to decipher, scores of them, hundreds, eventually thousands—Dostoyevsky, Proust, even Iris Murdoch, *The Waste Land*, Nietzsche, Simone de Beauvoir, very fleetingly Karl Marx. Indeed, Gide. There were biographies, histories of China and the Aztecs, explorers' tales from Africa, *Seven Years in Tibet*, Jung, books about super strings and black holes. Texts multiplied like bacteria under a microscope. I was left rudderless in a vast sea of bibles. In the end the world itself became a kind of multifarious text to puzzle out. We were warned of this, it must be said, countless times right from the start: if you Protestants are going to vest all authority in the Bible, with no popes or saints or holy relics, you'll end up either indifferent to God or sunk in unbelief. This is what will happen, Boileau warned, for instance, fulminating against the early French Reformers, once every man is his own pope with his Bible in his hand. A mere book will not be enough. He was quite right. Look at Scandinavia.

Every time I walk to the baker's or the post office near my house, the noticeboard in front of the local Baptist church invites me to come in and learn about Jesus, who, without any middleman, can apparently 'blot out' my transgressions. The Catholics, just up the street, simply advertise the time they celebrate mass. How telling. But there's a catch with the Baptists: to receive God's grace I must first believe in Him (and the Baptists, for reasons I've never been able to fathom—certainly none are given in the *text*—think Jesus *is* God). Well, having read what He has to say about Himself in the Holy Scriptures, I'm not at all sure that I now do believe in Him. I need other books. That's the trouble with being a Protestant: after scrambling towards modernity for several hundred years, we've now arrived to find that modernity isn't even Christian. Catholics may also scramble, but not forwards.

Protestant to the core, I still didn't think of myself as one. It took mass in the Cathedral in Oporto to make me do that. I might be a heathen, I thought to myself as I scampered downhill towards the river, but I am a Protestant heathen. In the early hours of the morning, around three or four, I might even be an atheist, but always a Protestant atheist. Late on a sunny afternoon, on the other hand, at the back of the house looking out on the garden, I'm inclined to mellow—at that time of day things don't look quite so black and white. But even then my mellowing is reasoned, sober, Protestant. Even then I accept that it's just me and Him (if He's there). Zigzagging down towards the water, dodging cats and grubby children tugging at my sleeve, I began to see in a flurry of small illuminations why I loved as I did, thought and talked as I did, joked, voted, ate, even decorated my living room and chose my shoes and socks (not to mention my companions) as I did: I was a Protestant.

As was André, of course, and he remained Protestant (if not, finally, a believer) despite the strenuous efforts of his friends and enemies to convert him to Catholicism. He refused to be 'gassed' by Rome, as he put it, although a surprising number of his friends succumbed to the fumes. He refused to bargain, as I refuse. The epiphany in Oporto took place before the episode with the caterpillar and the castle in Normandy. Still looking back, I'm surprised I didn't catch sight of Gide grinning at me from a doorway or an upper window even then as if to say: 'Ah! Something else you've finally understood!' (About him or about myself?) Sometimes, now I know him better, and given that our lives have followed such startlingly similar paths, I half-wonder (not that I believe in ghosts, but I don't know how else to put it) whether he was secretly following me, daring me to turn around and confront him, to admit that we were... what? *What*? We certainly weren't the *same*. Apart from anything else, I have no appetite for lissome youths. Well, no more than anybody else—obviously I can appreciate their beauty, I'm not blind, but I have no desire to frolic with them *à la* Gide, let alone ravish them. We had affinities, though, Gide and I. We were cut from the same cloth. Then I reached the bottom of the hill, emerging onto the astonishingly beautiful quayside by the river. Now I felt translucent, almost liquid. Drifts of rain came slowly up the narrow valley from the sea, turning the steep hillsides a yellowish grey. If a ship had been leaving for Goa, I'd have jumped aboard.

By the time all these memories had come tumbling out, Daniel and I were pulling up again back at Albert's house. The blue door flew open, he poked his head out for just a second and then disappeared inside again, no doubt to pop the kettle on. He'd be curious to know how we'd managed to amuse ourselves in Anduze.

5.

MOROCCO

Towards sunset, listening carefully to make sure that the hunters had gone, I set off up the road beside the stream into the wooded valley behind the house. I needed to have the sting taken out of the day. Almost nothing stirred—a dragonfly whizzed past, a hawk was circling slowly far above. All around me were the forests where the *camisards*—the Protestant rebels—had once heard angels sing. All I could hear was the croaking of a few frogs and the faint gurgle of water from the old stone mill opposite, but the hush perfumed with lavender and narcissus was soothing nonetheless. Relishing the solitude, I began talking aloud to myself. I know of no better way to tease apart tangled thoughts. What would the mosses and dragonflies care? Across the stream in the ancient monastery where Charlemagne had once heard mass (so they said), lights were coming on. The residents in their bijou apartments were probably considering a drink before dinner.

To be frank, by the time we got back to Albert's I was feeling a bit dispirited. The things I'd tried to explain to Daniel at the museum and on the drive home were precious to me, yet I wasn't sure he'd understood my feelings. I suppose he'd been distracted by the Pondicherry sideshow earlier in the day, but that's what happens when you travel with the young: their attention wanders, they flit about aimlessly and then stop and gawp. You have to be patient.

I wasn't jealous, not at all. As far as I was concerned, he was welcome to spend the rest of his life in Ma Thingo's ashram in Pondicherry, prostrate at her feet, muttering mindless incantations and eyeing off the other monks. Good luck to him. Anyway, it was hardly likely: he had a perfectly good job at the Louvre, something with a title that was gibberish to me and seemed to involve designing websites. No, it was his way of appearing to treat everything as a game that bothered me, always slipping out of my grasp, leaving me feeling earthbound and dull.

In addition, the undercurrent of hostility at the dinner table the night before towards someone I had a fellow feeling for troubled me—and I'd failed to defend him. Which meant that I'd failed to defend myself as well. There was something sanctimonious about so many of the accusations hurled at Gide—all this business about how 'distasteful' it was of Gide to 'trawl the boulevards' (as if Albert hadn't 'trawled' in his time, although obviously not boulevards, he hadn't had to, and not for boys). And all this pursed-lipped piety about 'boys' (as if they'd been innocents, as if right through history men—respected poets and writers Albert had on his own bookshelves—had not chosen younger beloveds to reward for certain favours). And Madeleine, a virgin until the day she died, abandoned at home in Cuverville, flicking dust off the banisters and reading *The Imitation of Christ* while her cruel husband gallivanted around Europe and Africa debauching the young—well, there were two sides to that story as well. But I'd failed miserably to stave off the attack, however playful it had been on the surface. I needed to sort out what I really thought.

It was like losing at a game of snakes-and-ladders: every time I tried climbing to a square near the top of the board—those sorties along the Paris boulevards, for instance, or to the bath houses, his obsession with North Africa, his botched marriage: what did I really think about these things?—I hit a snake and slid. Down I slithered from square to square: from Daniel's teasing remoteness to my own memories of Morocco decades earlier, to the Dostoyevsky he said I'd read too much of when I was young... And Dostoyevsky brought Tolstoy to mind (another snake) and so Levin in *Anna Karenina*, his head bursting from the shouting match raging inside it (Plato, Spinoza, Kant, Schelling, Hegel, Schopenhauer, all hammering away, shouting each other down)... and then the peasant Fyodor, who'd heard of none of these foreign pundits, telling Levin simply to 'remember God', and Levin striding away along the highway, *electrified*, reborn. Should I have mentioned Levin to Daniel? Had he ever read *Anna Karenina*? An avid reader, his tastes were eccentric. Slipping and sliding I hit the bottom: that moment when I took *If It Die* down from the shelf in that Sydney bookshop. Actually, even that was not at the very bottom of the board. Below '*Dear*, do you want the little musician?' was my mother gently telling me when I was nine or ten, while stirring the washing in the copper, that our neighbour, Mrs Fogg, could talk to me in an astounding new way about this 'God' I'd just told her I no longer believed in. And she did. Mrs Fogg was my Fyodor, and I was electrified, and to this day there's the occasional flash and shower of sparks, however many books I might read by today's great minds or boulevards I might saunter along, sharp-eyed.

But it wasn't right to the bottom that I slid as I walked, enveloped by a chorus of frogs, but to the square where Gide told Mrs Fogg to stay at home and hold her tongue: Morocco. In the middle of that square was a face: an olive-skinned, black-eyed, smiling face with delicately etched eyebrows.

I met Ahmed on a plane forty years ago, flying from

East Berlin to Prague on my first trip to Europe. Even in those days, under the Soviet boot, Prague was a beautiful city. Even then, at least for someone from the antipodes, a walk through old Prague and across the Charles Bridge to the castle on the hill was like drifting through a dream city. Everything I was in real life back at home began to slide backwards into shadow. Panic tinged with inexplicable excitement. The trouble was, I realised after a day or two, that Prague was not my particular dream. What I most vividly remember about Prague that foggy October is Ahmed.

Once I got home and Ahmed was back in Morocco, we began to write to each other. To this day I remember the almost voluptuous pleasure I felt whenever a letter from Ahmed was waiting for me in my letter box: the exotic stamps, the delicate airmail paper, the message from Morocco in faultless blue-inked French. There had been no particular intimacy between us in Prague, no casbah moment—I was not ready for one and Ahmed was by no means a penniless *caouadji* with not much else to offer—but I did picture him (of course I did—I'd read Gide) writing these letters to me as I read them. I could bring his lean, brown face and black eyes immediately to mind, a certain masculine playfulness and physical ease with himself that attracted me. As I remember, we mostly wrote to each other about politics. (At much the same age Gide advised himself to 'never engage in politics and almost never read the newspapers, but never miss an opportunity to talk politics with anyone whatsoever'.) Ahmed was a Muslim but a Marxist, which is why he'd been studying in East Berlin, while I was a Christian (from my point of view, although perhaps not the Archbishop of Canterbury's) with fairly conventional liberal ideas, about to study in Moscow. It was a complete mismatch, to tell the truth, but that was beside the point: Ahmed from Morocco was eros—not sex, but eros. Ahmed was the incarnation of my secret double self. I took a sudden and violent liking to him somewhere high over Dresden.

One's hidden double is by no means just a sexual being—it's much more intricate than that—although almost everything we read nowadays or watch on television suggests with a smirk that that's what it all boils down to. Gide, for instance, with his Protestant taste for duality in general, liked to play at feeling riven, but the dualities he had in mind were not chiefly sexual. He liked to claim to be both a northerner and a southerner (his mother being from Normandy, his father from the Huguenot south), to have both Catholic and Protestant roots (his mother's family having once been Catholic) and on one occasion, mischievously, to have been born 'between two stars', Scorpio and Sagittarius. He makes himself sound like Belgium. Most of us play these games with ourselves from time to time just to reassure ourselves that who we've turned out to be is not entirely our fault. He put his finger on a much more important duality in himself when he noted in his diary at the age of thirty-seven: 'I'm just a small boy having fun—doubling as a Protestant pastor who bores him.' In other words, a naughty little boy of thirty-seven coupled with a pastor who was beginning to lose his faith. The mortal and the immortal, the flesh and the spirit. Sex is only part of the story.

Sometimes you need to leave home to see this sort of duality for what it is. You need a vantage point, far from the habits of mind you've been nestling in, from which to look back with a fresh perspective at who you have been all your life. So when, after some months, Ahmed suggested I visit him in Morocco on my way to Moscow, I thought: why not?

In retrospect, I suspect that I went to Morocco at the age of twenty-two at least in part to live out the self that Gide had fashioned in me (although not created). Exactly what drew him to North Africa at twenty-three, rather than to Japan or Norway, it's hard to say, although there are some clues in his diary. (A visit to the sheltered valleys around La Roque, reeking of fecundity and families, gives you a good idea as well of why Tunis or Algiers might appeal to him in ways that Kyoto or Oslo wouldn't.) Six months or so before he set sail for Tunis with Paul Laurens he noted in his diary: 'Until the age of twenty-three I've lived a completely virginal and depraved life; crazed to such a point that eventually I was seeking everywhere some bit of flesh I could press my lips to.' A normal double life, in other words, for a teenager, although unusual in a Frenchman by the time he had reached the age of twenty-three. But why set sail for Tunisia instead of just taking the train to Paris?

A Thousand and One Nights, the book his father read to him when he was a child, must have played its part. Indeed, these Arabian stories were the first thing he thought of when he disembarked in Tunis. And his appetite for Africa had been whetted in Seville, where he'd 'hatched out' and 'come into flower', driven wild by the 'beauty of the people' as well as the scent of orange blossom. Seville was almost Africa, but not quite: it was still Christian—and he was travelling with his mother. Prague with Ahmed, I suppose, was my Seville.

Back from Spain, disoriented and excited, André had confided to his diary: 'Now my prayer (for it's still a prayer) is this: O God, let this too narrow morality of mine burst and let me live—oh, let me live fully; and oh, give me the strength to do so without fear, and without always thinking that I am about to sin!' This is what I can understand. This is a young man who is ready to let his two selves begin to merge—to stop living a double life. To do this, to leave your youth behind in this way, you must leave home (without your mother). Unless you do have a double life to stop leading, I must admit that I don't see much point in leaving home in the first place, except for a holiday.

At twenty-two I would not have had either the honesty or understanding to write the lines Gide wrote in his diary. I don't have any diaries or letters from that year to reread, but I'm sure that if I did come up with reasons for going to Morocco they'd have been carefully encrusted with high-minded flourishes my everyday self could comfortably live with: I'd have been going to broaden my horizons, learn about Moroccan culture, see Roman ruins . . . tourist brochure arguments, the lot of them. Gide was far more mature than I was at that age: 'The yearning to educate myself is my greatest temptation,' he wrote. 'If only I could live on some foreign shore where, the moment I stepped outdoors, I could delight in the sun, the wind and the infinite horizon of the sea!' In other words, he was consciously ready for unmediated pleasure. I wouldn't have known what the phrase meant.

As young André's ship approached the shores of Africa for the first time, he was almost delirious with expectation: 'Africa! I said this mysterious word over and over again to myself. I let it swell with terror, alluring terror, and with expectancy, and in the hot night I turned my eyes with desperate longing towards its promise, sweltering and swathed in flashes of lightning.' (A bit purple, but you know what he means.)

I'm not sure that flying into Rabat in 1966 was quite as exciting as Gide's arrival in Tunis in 1893, but then my memories have mostly faded or become frozen. All I have left is a few vignettes. Certainly there were no camels at Rabat airport (Gide was 'amazed' at the sight of all the camels on the wharf in Tunis); and the hustling crowd at the exit was not 'straight out of *A Thousand and One Nights*', although in parts of the medina they were. What I most vividly remember about Morocco now is not even the snake-charmers in Marrakech or the ill-lit alleyways in the fabulous souks in Fez; not the wilderness of the Atlas range or Roman columns and mosaic floors baking in the sun; but Ahmed's house. When you stepped inside the front door straight from the street, you found yourself immediately in a small, beautifully tiled room where visitors with no intimate connection with the family were served mint tea and perhaps a small almond cake—even a hooka (I was scandalised)—while they talked business with Ahmed's father. They'd once have brought with them a slender vial of perfume as a gift, even essence of orange blossom, perhaps, or jasmine, a coy gesture towards the intimacies hidden deeper inside the house—perhaps they still did. Even today in any souk in North Africa perfume sellers will press you to savour their array of fragrances and take away with you some precious essence stoppered with wax and wrapped in white tissue paper.

But for most visitors there was no question of penetrating beyond this 'parlour' into the courtyard and rooms beyond, where the women were, where the man you were talking to lived out another life or other lives. This was as far as you got.

When I passed into the inside courtyard I felt a surge of sensual pleasure, a small voluptuous tremor—I was intruding on a world screened off from strangers' eyes, a world of unveiled bodies, private emotions, loves, jealousies, anguish, joy. In the elegant sunlit courtyard, in the upstairs bedrooms, lined with perfume bottles, mirrors and hand-crafted cupboards, in the bathrooms, kitchen and hallways, the family was free to unmask itself, as much as any of us can.

As a child you can run all over the house or out into the street, you can be yourself anywhere, but once you've begun to grow up you learn the rituals of what is to be hidden and what can be revealed—and where. You are now literally a man of many parts.

I remember lounging on divans in the shade just off the inner courtyard, drinking mint tea and talking to Ahmed and his brothers; I remember the thrill of exploring this internal world of staircases, passageways and private rooms, each with a tiny latticed window affording glimpses of the sandy-white world outside; I remember standing on the roof amongst the washing, looking out at all the other roofs of Rabat, where figures swathed in all manner of flowing garments were sitting, playing, calling to each other, passing time in a strange half-world that was open to the sky—and to my eyes—yet at the same time mysteriously secluded. I'd never been in a house like this before. And I remember the call of the muezzin, as mysterious and menacing to me as church bells are to a Muslim.

Most vividly of all I remember the stirrings of desire, not so much for the slim nakedness under the djellabas and haïks, as for initiation into their way of being male. It baffled me, alarmed me and swept me off my feet. Ahmed, his brothers and his friends seemed to orientate themselves by a different compass. What was north and what was south? I ached to know.

In other words, what was not just exciting but intoxicating about being in Rabat was a sense of oblivion. Every night alone in my moonlit room I could recollect who I was supposed to be, but by day Morocco dazzled me. I could forget. I've never quite recovered.

To Ahmed and his friends, I think now, looking back, I was probably just a curiosity, a plaything that Ahmed had picked up in Europe, as it were. After a few days they tired of me, leaving me to my own devices. In the end I went off to the bus station without even saying goodbye, except to the servants. I never heard from Ahmed again. I wonder if in the intervening years I've ever even crossed his mind.

Another curious thing happened in Morocco, linking me in an unexpected way to André Gide. When I first arrived, all my luggage was sent on by mistake to Senegal, so I arrived in downtown Rabat from the airport not just stripped of my everyday self, but stripped of everything. Then I discovered that nobody could make sense of Ahmed's address, which I'd jotted down on a scrap of paper. Nobody at all—nobody I accosted in the teeming streets, not even the taxi drivers who in principle were willing to take me anywhere. I may have been unconsciously ready to leap into a vacuum, but this was too abrupt, too all-engulfing. 'The seething street does not become *unreal* to me exactly,' I wrote about that moment thirty years later, 'it becomes in the blink of an eye more what I'd call *relatively* real, and what I have to do is hook it up to a different relative reality, hovering above it. There's a meshing in the offing, I can feel it in my bones.'

So I walk out into the street and set off, following my nose, waiting for these two enactments of reality—what my eyes are seeing and what they still cannot—to mesh. My body is walking. *I* am stock-still.

Mumbo-jumbo, most people would say, mystical twaddle. (Not Mrs Fogg, though.) 'Flux' is what Daniel said when I told him. Be that as it may, when I stopped and asked a passer-by if he knew the address on my piece of paper, he said: 'Yes, of course I know it and I know that house because Ahmed is my nephew. I'll take you there now.' And he did.

Now, this sort of thing happens to me quite frequently, but especially when I travel, when I've been 'stripped' of my everyday self. But it's André Gide who seems to have effortlessly understood this kind of experience. I was stunned when I came across the following passage in his *Journal*. He's commenting here on why he seems to have difficulty in recognising people on sight (a difficulty I also experience). It has nothing to do with a lack of interest or attention, he says.

> I believe it comes ... from my lack of a certain *sense of reality*. I can be extremely sensitive to the outer world, but I never succeed completely in believing in it ... I can't get over a certain astonishment that things are as they are, and if they were suddenly different, it seems to me that that would hardly astonish me any more. For me the real world never stops being a little fantastic.

Then Gide tells the story of how he once watched his coachman slipping from his seat without saying a word, ending up dangling in the void about to fall under the wheels. 'I did not feel the slightest emotion,' he wrote, 'I was simply extraordinarily interested (*amused* would be more accurate),' although he was quick to grab the reins and avert an accident. What he felt was that he was 'taking part in it all as if at a show *outside of reality*' and would have felt exactly the same if it had happened to him rather than to the coachman. He couldn't 'take it seriously', although he was not just sensitive, but 'hypersensitive' to what was happening. He is not concerned with the question of whether or not he 'believes' in the outer world: 'it's the feeling of reality that I do not have. It seems to me that we are all actors in a fantastic parade and that what others call reality, their outer world, has no more existence than the world of [my novel] *The Counterfeiters* ...'

It's revealing, I think, that he compares the world

he feels so detached from with art. There's a paradox here, which many artists are disconcertingly conscious of: at the same time as everyday life loses its *meaning*, its *gravity* (although not its beauty or fascination)—any semblance of ultimate significance—you are intensely aware that every single syllable of what you write, every half-tone of what you paint, every demi-semiquaver of what you compose, is of *vital* importance. Every word, brushstroke or minim is packed with meaning, ready to erupt. Meanwhile, beyond the windows of your study or studio, the world goes its merry way, a parade of random vanities.

Some five years after explaining himself to himself like this, more or less at the age I am now, he tried to elucidate where this sense of unreality came from. Again, I think he cut straight to the heart of the matter. His Christian upbringing as a child, he now thinks, 'irremediably *detached* me from this world, inculcating in me, not so much . . . a disgust for this earth as a disbelief in its reality'. Few Christians these days, not even Protestants, will have the faintest idea what he was talking about, but I do. I think you have to grow up like that, I think you have to *experience* it, in order to understand. When I read the next few lines in his diary, my mind flew back immediately to my first day in Rabat. Without any metaphysical flim-flam, he goes straight to the nub of the matter:

> I have never succeeded in taking this life completely seriously. It's not that I have ever been able to believe (as far as I remember) in eternal life (I mean an afterlife), but rather I believe in another facet to this life, which escapes our senses and of which we can only be very imperfectly aware . . . An indefinable impression of being 'on tour' and of playing in makeshift sets with cardboard daggers.

Right at the end of his life (he was eighty), in his very last book, *So Be It* or *The Chips are Down*, the most serenely random of all his books, he mentions 'surprising myself yesterday wondering with complete seriousness if I was still really alive. The outer world was there and I was perceiving it with marvellous clarity, but was it really I who was perceiving it?' I have a way to go before I hit eighty, but I've been seized by a similar perception many times—you can be just sitting reading a book or making soup and it strikes you like a flash of lightning through the open window: without warning and for no apparent reason you feel like an absence, not a presence, like a ventriloquist's doll. But who in that case is the ventriloquist? As Schopenhauer—and Gide—remarked, the young, if metaphysically inclined, are likely to see themselves as the ventriloquist, animating the entire universe. 'Nothing existed except as a function of myself,' Gide wrote about himself at the age of eighteen. 'Now the question was turning around: without my help everything existed and continued to be . . . *I absented myself*; it seemed to me that I was no longer there and my disappearance passed unnoticed.'

On the face of it, this is precisely the sort of thing that Oscar Wilde might have wished for the young Frenchman with the mask-like face when he first met him at one of Mallarmé's Tuesdays: the loss (as the post-modernists might put it) of 'an authentic unified subject'—of a self, a soul, of anything below the changing surface. Oscar would have been tickled pink—at least until he converted to Catholicism. But he'd have been mistaken in his glee: Gide hadn't turned into Oscar Wilde in old age at all. There is still a ventriloquist, there is still something real beneath the surface.

I thought I might try to find some of these passages for Daniel to read when I got home—Albert was sure to have *So Be It* somewhere on his bookshelves, half the walls in the house were covered in books—and see what he made of them. Perhaps this would be something he'd quickly understand and take seriously. Perhaps it was something we could share. But when I came scrunching up the drive after my walk, Albert and Daniel were in deep conversation under the nettle-tree above the stream. The smell of apricots stewing in lemon and nutmeg was wafting across from the kitchen window. Drawing closer, I heard Albert say something about 'the Two giving birth to the Three and the Three giving birth to . . .' something or other (I can never remember the detail of this kind of spiritual kitsch) and the moment passed. With the old monastery catching the last rays of the sun across the stream behind them, they looked enviably serene.

◆

On leaving Rabat, I crisscrossed Morocco until I reached Tangier, on buses, trains, even hitchhiking. By the time I flew off to Moscow, although I'd had no 'casbah' experience, strictly speaking, leaving my soul and body so light I almost blew away, I had held a few 'wild, fervent, lascivious and saturnine' young bodies in my naked arms. On the beach in Tangier in those days, for instance, even before the sun went down, or amongst the abandoned Roman ruins at Volubilis, in parks at sunset, at the back of djellaba shops where I'd been sweet-talked into trying on garments in the blues and greens I loved, even in half-empty youth hostels after they were locked down for the night, lean young men would draw close and coax me, sometimes fiercely, to come and find a corner where we could melt into each other and give each other bliss. There was no exchange of passwords, as there would have been at home, no long drawn out dance of glances, gestures and other antics—it was very straightforward: just a few conversational knick-knacks, really, thrown in the air to attract my attention and then the offer of friendship with no holds barred. What astounded me was the way their cocky maleness—so sharp, so conventionally hard-edged—could kaleidoscope every few minutes into something else: goatish, cheeky, tender, sultry, warm, merciless, inviting, brutal. A man intent on utter intimacy could obviously be many more things (with other men) than I'd thought possible.

By the time I left for Moscow I had, in a sense, grown up. I was aching for feminine company (wall-to-wall virility is tiring); but, more importantly, like Gide on *his* first trip to North Africa, over a year before he met Oscar Wilde in Algiers, I was ready at last to think about marriage. In those days you got married, as the men in the Moroccan bazaars and the laneways of Sousse still do. Finding the right woman to love, given the newfound gamut of your desires and affections, was not a straightforward matter; but it was easier if you'd at least gone up and down the scale a few times before you started looking. Gide had no need to look: he'd picked his cousin Madeleine Rondeaux out of the crowd when he was just thirteen. I dare say in both our cases it was a mismatch. Neither of us, though, would ever admit that, in the context of the times and places we lived in, we'd done the wrong thing.

6.

CUVERVILLE

'Madeleine,' I said as we came to a jolting halt.
　　'Yes,' said Miriam. 'One more stop.'
　'No, not the station, I meant Gide's wife. Seeing madeleine written up like that reminded me of her.'
　'Ah, yes. Poor Madeleine.'
　We gazed out of the window. It was late. Late in the evening in the Paris metro there's an unsettling subterranean feel to the platforms and corridors, as if at any moment hordes of the damned are about to come flooding in, bent on mischief. You can hardly wait to get out. Madeleine. Stark black tiles on white. The name that Gide said meant to him 'grace, gentleness, intelligence and kindness'. No other woman on earth had the right to a name so redolent of goodness. When it came to his wife, Gide had a bad case of angelism.

The vast billboards lining the platform leered at us through the window. *je ne suis pas jolie*, the Kookaï model pouted, *je suis pire*. ('I'm not pretty, I'm worse.') Oozing virility right next to her were three basketball players in white suits by De Fursac, all ferociously handsome, two of them black. You could almost smell their hard-edged maleness wafting into the carriage. Up and down the station, everywhere you looked, were images of wantonness, the promise of fleeting ecstasy. Yet right opposite our window a woman was joyfully kissing a rosy child perched on a stepladder, reminding us that it would soon be Mother's Day: *vivent les mamans!* the poster crowed. She too was electrifyingly beautiful. The Galeries Lafayette was trying to have it both ways. As most of us do.

'All the things Madeleine Gide never had,' I mused aloud. 'It's ironic.'

'What do you mean?'

'All this,' I said, gesturing vaguely at the billboards now sliding past us as we gathered speed. 'Sex, motherhood . . . fun.' The woman who wasn't pretty but worse flew by again. A final madeleine and the tunnel swallowed us up. 'These are creatures from a different planet. She'd have been dumbfounded.'

'She must've had *some* sex at *some* point,' Miriam said briskly. 'How long were they married?'

'Over forty years. But no, none at all, as far as anyone knows.'

'What about while he was away? Which seems to have been most of the time.'

'Certainly not! Her God was a jealous one.' Miriam, who doesn't have a god, jealous or otherwise, having had a surfeit of them in Sri Lanka, looked no less puzzled. 'But that's not quite what I meant. I meant that what we just saw—what we see on every station we pass through—would have struck her as an unbelievably brazen invitation to sin.'

'Sin,' she said. In the swishing darkness of the tunnel we briefly savoured 'sin' as we might some strange Amazonian fruit we'd read about in travellers' tales but never tasted in all its sweet-smelling lusciousness. 'This woman is beginning to interest me very much.'

'Saint Lazare, this is us.' We stepped out onto the platform in front of a poster advertising group tours to Morocco. *maroc. circuit grand sud. a partir de 638€.* The main station on the street above us was where Gide used to arrive from Normandy, as it happens, on his way to North African circuits of his own, but, needless to say, he never went there with the herd and the cost was something he simply never had to consider. He was not just well-off, he was rolling in it. Old Rondeaux money, all of it, made from the manufacture of calico. As an only child he'd inherited his mother Juliette Rondeaux's entire fortune in money and land, including La Roque-Baignard, while his wife inherited her share of her father Emile Rondeaux's estate, including

Cuverville. As landowners, he and Madeleine had peasants, most of whom probably never got as far as Rouen, let alone Morocco.

'I wonder if Zaïda would fancy spending another Sunday in Normandy,' I mused as we made our way up to the street.

'Oh, I think she could be persuaded. What did you have in mind?'

'Cuverville. I'd like to see Madeleine's château at Cuverville. I'd like to see where they spent their married life together. It's where he fell in love with her.'

'He fell in love with her?'

'All right—"began to love her", then. Is that better? Even that's not quite right: he first became infatuated with her at the Rondeaux house in Rouen when she accidentally found out about her mother's affair. You can imagine how scandalous, how devastating that was in a pious household like the Rondeaux'.'

'Infatuated... is that all?'

'Enraptured, *drunk* with love for her. Well, not for *her*, not for his actual cousin, but for the angelic being he took her to be. He wanted to protect her from life's anguish. But love in the quieter sense flowered at Cuverville.'

Cuverville—Gide was always arriving at Cuverville or leaving it, every time you turn a page of his diaries there it is again: Cuverville. The tall black men we were passing in the corridor were playing something jumpy on drums and xylophone, something that should have made me think of the desert after sunset. And ever since I'd got back from Tornac I'd been plotting my own Grand Circuit Sud to Algiers, Biskra, Sousse and the Sahara in increasingly vivid detail. All I could think of, though, as we rose towards the street was bees in the wisteria blossoms at Cuverville; Gide working in the garden behind the house or sitting with just his slippered feet in the sun, happiness rising in him like warm sap (he said); his piano practice, too—hours of it, Chopin, Schumann, Beethoven; and all those books he read, sometimes aloud to himself (Dickens, Nietzsche, Turgenev, Balzac, Rimbaud, Latin poets . . . and dozens of writers I've never heard of). And I thought of how over the years languor had slowly turned into torpor, of Cuverville 'sleeping in a cloud', as he once wrote, the climate there eventually 'shrinking and strangling' the writing he'd begun with passion in sultrier places in the south. After over thirty years of married life, he was writing of the strange feeling of numbness of the mind, of the will, of his whole being, which he rarely experienced anywhere except at Cuverville. ('I hang on here with the painful feeling that I'm sacrificing my work, my life, to her only because I love her.') Part of the problem, as he hinted himself a few years later, was no doubt that 'in the whole district there is not a single young or handsome creature to smile at or let my gaze linger on'. What can he have meant by that? Not just no likely lads, presumably, but not even anything to jog the memory. I had to see Cuverville.

'We could have lunch in Fécamp,' I said as we came out into the chilly garishness of the rue de Rome. 'More mussels—it's on the Channel.'

'Fécamp!' Miriam said with one of her small smiles. 'Irresistible.' She'd clearly never been there.

'And if you like cemeteries...' 'Oh, I love cemeteries.'

'Well, we can visit their graves in the village graveyard.' I don't much like cemeteries myself, they have a stagnant feel to them that I find uninviting. It would never even occur to me to wander around London's Highgate or Père Lachaise in Paris, for instance, peering at the tombstones of the famous, as so many people like to do. I can't see the point of it. I can't see what it helps you understand. I don't think I have much aptitude at all for the pilgrimage. For some reason, though, visiting the Gides' graves in a small, village churchyard with Miriam and Zaïda did quite appeal to me. 'Only, if we go,' I said, 'this time I'll be in charge of the map. It's disconcerting driving around with somebody at the wheel who believes in fate.'

'Oh, Zaïda doesn't believe in anything.' 'Exactly. They're the worst.'

♦

Soon after Madeleine Gide died, just before the outbreak of the Second World War, André wrote in his memoir *Et nunc manet in te* about how, whenever he'd come home to Cuverville, she would not be waiting with other members of the household on the front steps of the manor to greet him, but would be standing alone inside in the shadows of the entrance hall, weeping. Each time he would think of Coriolanus returning to Rome, wounded, from his exploits at Corioli. 'My gracious silence, hail!' Coriolanus says to his wife. 'Wouldst thou have laugh'd had I come coffin'd home,/ That weep'st to see me triumph? Ah, my dear,/ Such eyes the widows in Corioli wear,/ And mothers that lack sons.'

Madeleine *was* in some ways a widow—or as good as. And she was a mother lacking sons. Her husband's literary triumphs did often make her weep, too, not being the sort of triumphs her piety would have wished for him, even though all his novels were part of a conversation with her. (Not his last novel, *The Counterfeiters*—that was part of a conversation with his other enduring love, Marc Allégret.) A 'gracious silence'—or mostly gracious—more or less sums it up. Picturing her waiting for him in that vestibule, greeting him wordlessly, I find myself remembering something else Gide wrote about her in that memoir: the expression on her face, he said, in a photograph taken when she was just a girl was one of *étonnement craintif*—a kind of fearful astonishment at what adult life held for her. He'd hoped to wash it away with his overflowing joy in her presence, but failed.

This was not a good marriage, yet it was a great and enduring love. It happens all the time. It's heartbreaking. Why must the one be so often yoked to the other?

We'd arrived at the château in high spirits that Sunday. Zaïda was in a particularly jaunty mood because she almost never arrived at where she set out for, or at least not in one go. 'How *fecund!*' we'd exclaimed to each other, winding up through the hills towards Cuverville from the coast. '*Comme c'est fecund!*' (We were mocking Fécamp, the grim port town where we'd just had lunch. It deserved it.) In fact, this part of Normandy, Caux, is much less fecund than the Calvados region where Gide had spent his childhood. Windswept wheatfields, low hills a muted green, small copses of beech, stony villages of priggish-looking houses; but we didn't let any of this, not even the heavy, mauvish clouds rolling in from the Channel, dampen our mood. We sprang gaily from the car when we got to the ruined gates of the château, thrilled to have found it at last, hidden away behind its towering beech trees on the outskirts of a tiny village in the middle of nowhere. Yet the moment we saw the house across the lawn—long, reddish, two-storeyed, severely symmetrical—we all fell silent. It was like staring at a tombstone. Nothing stirred.

'It's not really a castle, either, is it,' Miriam said eventually. 'It's a big house.'

'I'm sure it was yellower in Gide's day,' I said, trying

to recall old photographs, 'and this lawn was less bare. There were more trees and bushes.'

'It certainly looks rather forbidding.' With her delicate fingers Miriam swathed herself more tightly in her crimson shawl.

With its ten shuttered windows to the left of the pediment and ten to the right, and a line of dormer windows in its high, slate-grey mansard roof, the house stared back at us, expressionless, unmoved by our small burst of joy. But I knew its secrets—Gide and his friends revealed all of them in their writings. What we were looking at beyond the empty lawn was the pivot of his adult life, the unchanging, still centre he wheeled and swooped around in great nomadic loops of renewal, swinging out as far as Moscow, the Nile and the jungles of the Congo, then reeling himself in to come to rest again here, in this house, Madeleine's inheritance, by her side. This was his hearth. It could almost be said that Madeleine herself was his hearth rather than his wife.

'Perhaps,' Miriam said in her usual tart way, 'she'd have preferred to be his wife.'

If so, she married the wrong man. She married a man who simply forgot to ask himself if that might be the case until it was too late. Blind to her 'horrible suffering', as he eventually admitted to his dear friend Maria Van Rysselberghe (but not to Madeleine), he had built his happiness on her unhappiness. 'When I think of the mother that she could have been, even the lover! I have been odious.' Yet, according to Gide, he and Madeleine never discussed it—not, I suppose, that he could have done much about it if they had. Carnal love, as he called it, had never been what he was offering her. There was no agreement that he never would: it was simply never discussed. A century ago a woman's expectations in this regard rarely were. Madeleine, he wrote, was 'all soul' for him—sex didn't come into it. This was certainly unusual—as a rule there's at least a quiver of desire at some point early on, even if it soon becomes apparent that the attraction is at root not sensual—but it's not unheard-of. And, if he's to be believed, she didn't once openly complain, or not, at least until the burnt letters incident in 1918. She accepted the situation, it seems, with disappointment and 'mute resignation', eventually taking refuge in religion, household chores and good works amongst the poor, of whom there was no lack. Although she lived with Gide, and undoubtedly loved him, believing that she had had 'what was finest' in him, she felt more and more married to God.

'I don't believe it,' Miriam said. 'Not a word in forty years?'

'Forty-three.'

'Didn't he feel guilty?'

'No, I don't think he ever did. Regretful, sad, furious with himself for being so blind, but not guilty.'

'He sounds like a monster.'

No, Miriam, I'd have liked to say, as she turned away to look for Zaïda, he wasn't a monster, and she was no saint, it was more complicated—and interesting—than that. Left standing at the fence, gazing at the blank oblong across the grass, I felt as usual that I should be defending him for some reason, but hardly knew how to start. Yet I felt I *understood*, I understood why André wanted to marry his cousin Madeleine, especially after his youthful adventures in North Africa, why they loved each other and why, despite their love, they caused each other such misery during their marriage, yet never parted. It's not a marriage that can be judged by modern expectations of that arrangement. Nowadays if you're not the 'marrying kind' you don't marry. In those days you did and made the best of it. This resulted in a very singular union. André Gide was a very singular man. At some point in his adolescence, it seems to me, André came to see his cousin Madeleine as his salvation. You are the being, we say to ourselves when this sort of perception begins to dawn on us, who will be the guarantee of my goodness, whatever I might do. More than that: you are the *only* being I know who can guarantee it. This not only makes you beautiful in my eyes, this is what beauty *means*, even in music and paintings. Without you, without knowing that you will always be there as the very touchstone of who I really am, I fear I will permanently forget who I am, fly apart, cease to exist. You will not change me, mind, but anchor me. (Gide used this word of Madeleine: he spoke of her being 'anchored' at Cuverville.) And in return I will bring you whatever joy I can, in abundance. In a word, you will be a sort of *hyperpresence* (to borrow one French critic's illuminating description of Madeleine). You will abide with me while I go adventuring in the world and be a comfort to me when I am at home. To me it's perfectly understandable that after his straightlaced, adolescent notion of his own goodness had started to come unstuck in North Africa he should have rushed home to marry Madeleine—not just marry, but marry Madeleine, the incarnation of his disappearing goodness. However, she was a woman, not some ethereal hyperreality. He wounded her by abandoning her constantly to go adventuring and then writing up his depraved adventures for all the world to read. She wounded him by turning Cuverville into some kind of joyless convent. So the marriage came unstuck along with his goodness. But I understand the impulse.

Now, this is not the kind of mating—with a dash of feeling—that marriage is supposed to be all about. This is obviously not the sort of 'love' we read about in novels or see acted out on screen. This is not what Antony felt for Cleopatra, at least in Shakespeare's version, what Vronsky, or even crusty old Karenin, felt for Anna Karenina, what Rhett Butler felt for Scarlett O'Hara, or all those coltish young lads in the television soaps presumably feel for their pretty-doll girlfriends.

Hyperpresences are too unearthly, too undramatic, to weave stories out of, they don't promise a climax of any kind, they don't incite narrative thrust. In a way, their whole point lies in their refusal to get involved in day-to-day narratives. Certainly, no young man nowadays would bother marrying one. Why would he? The authorities have no interest in them, while the family expects marriage to produce children. There's something boyish about the whole thing, really, something not quite manly, as if André and those like him (including quite a few of his fictional heroes) wanted to stay boys forever, spending their lives playing exciting games with other boys. It's reminiscent of all those young men—shadowy great-uncles on the fringes of old family photographs—who once upon a time courted their fiancées for years on end until eventually they died ('tragically', as a rule) doing something intrepid far, far away, usually with other young men. Wars and the colonies were a boon to them.

It may not be what's expected of a healthy young man, but it's not a crime, it's not even morally reprehensible, not in itself. Any number of men have friends they love on the one hand and friends they play with on the other. Any number of men have shied away from getting married, from committing themselves, in Robert Louis Stevenson's words, to trudging side by side with a wife and children down the road lying 'long and straight and dusty to the grave'. After all, once you're married, 'there is nothing left for you, not even suicide, but to be good'. It's a terrifying prospect. What man wants to stay good forever? But what if you want to get married like everyone else (it makes you so much easier for society to cope with), be naughty when it suits you, yet (miraculously) stay *fundamentally* 'good'? This is where a wife who is a hyperpresence is a godsend. What a loving hyperpresence can do in these circumstances, apart from being your safe harbour when you come home between escapades, is to serve as an abiding guarantee (like some mothers, really, or the Catholic Church) of your redeemability, of your essential virtue, whatever mischief you may get up to away from home. Since he wasn't a Catholic and had no mother by the time he married (significantly, he proposed to Madeleine just two weeks after his mother died), Madeleine must have seemed the perfect person to fulfil this role in Gide's life. Was she not an 'angel', as he kept calling her (a common incarnation of a hyperpresence and not at all the same thing as a saint), numbed at the age of fifteen by the discovery that her mother had a lover (with whom she later ran away to Paris)? As an erotically numbed angel, she herself may well have thought a man with no carnal intentions a felicitous choice, at least at the beginning. As she wrote to him soon after their engagement, it was not death that she feared, but marriage. To be frank, the more I learn about Madeleine from what Gide and his many biographers and friends wrote about her, the more I suspect that she was less an 'angel' than a woman who was terrified of the material world, which she barricaded out. She was impregnable. She found even a trip to nearby Fécamp daunting.

This, I'm sure, is why Gide could write with a perfectly straight face after Madeleine's death that 'it did not seem to me that I was unfaithful to her while seeking away from her a satisfaction of the flesh which I did not know how to ask of her'. You can't give your *heart* to anyone else—that would clearly be infidelity, and when Gide did this the result was catastrophic—but the odd orgasm with a stranger deprives a true hyperpresence of absolutely nothing, it's not even worth reporting. That's what being 'hyper' means. A hyperpresence is literally above it all. I know because, more anxious, like Gide, about my goodness than my virtue, I have had one for almost half my life now. I met mine a century after Gide met his, and mine is a man, not a woman, so everything is more straightforward. A hyperpresence is not a love object. It is the very air you breathe.

There is nothing inherently wrong with any of this, it seems to me, not even with wanting to stay a boy all your life, mucking about with other boys, if your wife or companion is in on the deal. There is nothing necessarily namby-pamby, either, by the way, about the desire to remain a boy all your life—every second famous explorer you can think of, trekking up the Nile or circumnavigating the globe, not to mention all those celebrated authors of children's stories, from J.M. Barrie to Edward Lear, seems to have been caught in the same dream.

On the contrary, many of these men were flamboyantly virile (the Earl of Rochester springs to mind) although not J.M. Barrie or Edward Lear. If it's to work well, though, the hyperpresence must be made aware of what sort of arrangement she's letting herself in for.

At first glance, this is where André Gide seems to have behaved inexcusably. If he had to get married, why on earth couldn't he have taken Madeleine aside one morning and explained that marriage of the normal kind was something he had no gift for (perhaps in the small, walled garden behind the house where the vegetable plots were?). We couldn't see the garden from where we stood that blustery afternoon, but I knew it was there. It's in *Strait is the Gate*, it's where, after a long separation, Alissa (who merges with Madeleine in my mind, although Gide keeps protesting that she is *not* Madeleine, just 'a point of departure' for the portrait he paints) waits for Jerome (who, presumably, is also *not* André). It's April in *Strait is the Gate* and along the pathways the shrubs are in luxuriant flower—lilacs, laburnums, weigelas, roses, all pinks and mauves and yellows. When Jerome arrives to look for Alissa, whom he wants to marry, his joy is like the sky, he says: 'warm, bright, delicately pure'. It's hard to think of a better metaphor for a hyperpresence than a warm, bright, delicately pure sky, just timelessly there, all-embracing, life-giving, as close as the air we breathe, yet so far above us that nothing we do in our daily lives can scar it. Both André and Madeleine loved this garden on the western side of the house, sometimes spending whole days there from dawn to dusk tending it devotedly. This is where he should have taken Madeleine one warm afternoon and explained to her about warm, bright, delicately pure skies.

The drawing room, with its polished mahogany furniture and honey-coloured parquet flooring, would not have done at all. Everything smelt of beeswax and turpentine, everything gleamed, it would have felt like a consultation at the doctor's. Nor would the dining room, with its three wicker chairs in front of the fireplace... better, but still too varnished, too mirror-bright, too Madeleine. André's own rooms above the kitchen would not have been suitable, either. They were too cluttered, with books and clothes piled up on chairs and washstand as if he were just camping there. Far too André. No, it would have had to be the garden. But it never happened. In forty-three years it never happened. Surely this is inexcusable.

He should have done it. He should have brought the subject up. Instead, one by one he gave her his books to read. Now, although there's no indication that she enjoyed them, I think he could be excused for believing that he'd explained himself in them fairly clearly. Five years before they married, for instance, he sent her a copy of his *Cahiers d'André Walter* (*André Walter's Notebooks*), which he'd begun writing as a teenager, together with his first proposal of marriage. In this book André tells his beloved Emmanuèle: 'I do not desire you. Your body is an embarrassment to me, and I have always been horrified by physical possession.' So which way the wind was blowing should have been fairly clear from the start.

Although *Fruits of the Earth* was published after they were married, he was still writing it at the time of their wedding. You would have to be not just naïve, as Madeleine undoubtedly was, but practically obtuse, which she wasn't, not to pick up the clues scattered about in this feverish tirade on happiness. She may not have known who Hafez was (the epigraph to Book I is from this Persian love poet who, 'reeling with love', was given to penning ecstatic *ghazels* in praise of waiters 'in the bloom of belovedness' whom he kissed 'full upon the mouth and lip'). She may not have known much about Virgil, either, for that matter, let alone caught the Virgilian echoes in the name Menalcas (the narrator's mentor in *Fruits of the Earth*, modelled on Wilde) who weans children from their families, 'making their hearts sick with longing for fruit that is wild and sour, with curiosity for strange loves': Menalcas whose 'soul was the inn standing open at the crossroads; whoever wished to enter, did so'; Menalcas who claimed to love 'neither man nor woman', but friendship, affection or love itself; Menalcas who went down with sailors to the ill-lit alleyways of the ports he frequented and set sail with three friends, a crew of sailors and four cabin-boys, 'falling in love with the least handsome of the four' and enjoying his gentle caresses, although less than he enjoyed the wild waves tossing the ship. But you don't have to know much about Hafez and Virgil, or anything about their passion for dusky cupbearers and piping shepherd lads, to get the drift. 'Love' in *Fruits of the Earth* is something that simply gushes—it's mirrored in all the streams, waves, fountains and running water lacing the book. Loving is like drinking—drinking moonlight. In other words, it's not about possession, but experiencing. It quite emphatically has nothing to do with the feelings a grown man has for his wife. Yet, according to Gide, Madeleine was simply surprised that her André could have written a book which 'was so unlike' him. It beggars belief.

Blind to what he'd so plainly written, she seems to have been wilfully blind to the implications of his behaviour as well. On their honeymoon, for example, which, with superb irony, retraced backwards his first trip to North Africa, although he made no attempt to hide from her his excitement when swarms of *ragazzi* surrounded their carriage in the villages they were trundling through in Northern Italy, Madeleine, he says, was simply 'surprised', feeling 'cut out of the game', 'kept at arm's length'. Did she not ask herself what exactly it was about her husband's excitement that surprised her?

Further south in Rome he not only ogled the delectable young men from Saraginesco offering themselves as 'models' on the Spanish Steps, but actually abandoned Madeleine to wander the city by herself while he took the pick of the bunch up to their apartment on the pretext of photographing them. (These sessions in the apartment on the Piazza Barberini probably took place two years later, rather than on their honeymoon, as he claimed in a fit of self-mortification, but this hardly makes them less shocking.) Astonishingly, he showed her the photographs, although not, to be sure, the 'more successful ones'. Even Gide suspected that she was in no more doubt about what was going on than all the young lads from Saraginesco were.

When they reached Algeria (and, again, this was probably on a later trip than he claimed) his behaviour on the train from Biskra to Algiers was so outrageous that even Madeleine was shocked. At each of the many stops along the way, the three schoolboys in the next compartment, half-naked in the suffocating heat, would lean out of their window, allowing Gide, in full view of his wife, and presumably of the crowds milling on the platform, to lean out of his own window and 'fondle the downy, amber-coloured flesh' of their arms. They enjoyed the game enormously, apparently. (Where the myth of adolescent sexual guilelessness comes from it's hard to imagine.) Sitting down again in his own compartment, Gide was left 'gasping for breath' with excitement. Madeleine said he'd made himself look like either a criminal or a madman. Perhaps 'criminal' was her roundabout way of calling a spade a spade.

In short, I would have thought that Gide's inclinations were almost scandalously obvious from the time he was an adolescent. All the same, he should have taken her into the garden they both loved so much one sunny afternoon and talked to her about the kind of love for her that he was capable of and the kind he was not. He wouldn't even have needed to speak about skies and angels, let alone hyperpresences. He could have found comfortingly Christian things to say, for instance, and he'd have been speaking in all sincerity: he could have alluded to his honest belief that his disembodied love for her was purer than the common or garden kind, undefiled as it was by any fleshly desire. He could have explained to her that in his dreams she was 'unembraceable'—*insaisissable*, as he once expressed it—so physically elusive as to be impossible to lay hold of (unlike schoolboys' arms). A presence, not a body. That would have put God in a spot: on the one hand Gide was not behaving as a Christian husband should, but on the other hand He now had Madeleine Rondeaux more or less all to Himself, which is the way He claims to prefer it. The conversation may have turned out to be inexpressibly distressing to both André and Madeleine, but much less distressing, surely, than spending a lifetime together not talking about it.

It wasn't until they'd been married for some twenty years or more that things came to a head. That's a long time. Early in the summer of 1917, during a lengthy stay in Paris away from his ideal wife, Gide at last found the ideal friend, somebody he could give his heart and mind to, with some degree of physical intimacy, someone he could both love and play with. In a word, at the age of forty-seven he fell in love. At the age of forty-seven, especially if it's for the first time, falling in love is a serious business. In an outburst of controlled rage Madeleine punished her husband in a way so exquisitely painful that it marked him for the rest of his life: she burnt every letter he'd ever written to her. Yet, incredibly, even then they didn't sit down together and lay their cards unambiguously on the table.

'Zaïda's disappeared.' It was Miriam, wrenching me back into the present. The mist had turned to light rain. The first thing I thought, as happens at such moments, was that Zaïda was forty-seven as well ... but I quickly refocused. 'You don't think ...' She didn't finish the sentence. Yes, I did think. Empty lawn, empty roadway—it was entirely possible Zaïda had gone ferreting about behind the house. As we both knew, it was possible that she was scaling the garden wall at that very moment. Or sitting up having coffee in the drawing room with the present owner of the house (also a widow). Princesses, even those in jeans, have trouble grasping the notion that some things are simply not permitted.

As it turned out, she hadn't got very far at all: after scouting around in the drizzle for a while we found her in a barn, talking to a ruggedly handsome man stacking wood with his two sons. (That's the other thing about princesses as opposed to queens: they can and do happily talk to anyone at all. Farmers, prime ministers, waiters, film stars—they're all much of a muchness to a princess.) He was regaling her with village gossip both about the Gides, who had died before he was born, and the resident widow, whom he claimed to know very well. Zaïda was all ears. His young sons just stood there, their eyes out on stalks. Although he knew the Gides had been 'famous', he seemed quite puzzled as to why anyone would come from Paris, let alone from half way across the world, to stare at a house.

'I don't suppose there's any way we could go around behind the house,' Zaïda said, 'it would be fascinating to see the garden.'

'It's not particularly interesting,' he said. 'It's just a garden.'

'But we'd love to see the gate,' Miriam said.

'The gate?'

'The gate from *Strait is the Gate*. It's in the wall.'

He looked at her as if she was batty. 'The gate's locked,' he said. His sons were watching with rapt attention as if we were a puppet show. Their father returned to stacking wood. I had the feeling that the show was coming to an end.

'Let's go and find the churchyard,' I said brightly, 'and pay our respects.' It looked as if the view across the lawn was about as close as we were going to get to Cuverville.

'You can't miss it,' said the ruggedly handsome farm-hand, 'it's on the road into the village.' He clearly didn't know much about Zaïda.

◆

'But this is a Catholic church,' Miriam said, when we pulled up beside the tiny stone building in the nearby village. On top of its tiny grey steeple there was definitely a cross. 'Surely he didn't convert on his deathbed, did he?'

'Certainly not,' I said. 'By the time he died he'd stopped believing in anything.'

'Still, sometimes, just as a bit of last-minute insurance ... Oscar Wilde, Voltaire ...'

'Gide never bargained. In fact, as I remember, the most appalling scandal erupted when a pastor appeared out of nowhere and spoke at his funeral. Heated arguments around the coffin, barbed comments in the press next day ...' Gide loathed funerals of any kind, agreeing with Jesus: 'Let the dead bury the dead.' 'To be honest,' I admitted, 'I can't see that it matters very much. A pastor, no pastor—what does it matter? Still, if his friends felt that he'd been betrayed . . . To tell you the truth, I'm never quite sure who funerals are for, anyway. Are you going to have one?'

'Well, I don't want my death to go unnoticed.' Well, no. Anyway, now he was here somewhere, side by side with his Protestant wife, stretched out under a gravestone in a Catholic churchyard. Perhaps there was a corner for agnostics and other renegades. It was just a matter of going slowly up and down the rows till we found him.

As usual I felt absolutely nothing as I read the names and epitaphs on the wet tombstones we passed, but Zaïda and Miriam were in their element, reading out the names to each other (and some were names to savour), commenting on the untimely deaths and building up a web of connections between the clans. All I could see was stones. And then finally, in the corner of the graveyard closest to the house just across the fields, Zaïda found them. She waved to us, gold bracelet glinting in a burst of sunlight. We scrunched across the gravel and stood in silence at the foot of the stones. A stillness touched us like a spell. There was nothing stagnant about this stillness, though, it was boundless—I'll never forget it—the kind of stillness that engulfs you when you open a window in a dark room and to your astonishment can see all the way to the horizon.

On Madeleine's stone on the right there was a Christian cross, her name, her date of birth and two lines of hope: *Blessed are the peacemakers: for they shall be called the children of God* from the Sermon on the Mount, and, just below that, from Revelation, *Blessed are the dead which die in the Lord from henceforth.* In French it reads '*Happy are the peacemakers . . .*' and '*Happy are the dead . . .*' which, in Madeleine's case, verged on mockery, surely.

On André's stone there were just two words: andre gide, and the dates of his birth and death. Yet the blankness of the pink-grey stone—how is this possible?—was at the same time an illusion. On this empty slate there were words, thousands of them, millions, words from the web of stories in our memories of him—even faces and landscapes seemed to be etched on the stone, clustering there as I looked—prayers, pleas, love letters, Alis, Mohammeds, hammams, Madeleine, Marc, minarets, deserts, Dostoyevsky, Cuverville, Virgil's shepherds, Olivier, Lafcadio, the Immoralist . . . that voice of his in all his books, seductive but knowing, sharp-edged . . . and all those conversations, a lifetime of them, piling up thick and fast when he was young, from snatches on dark boulevards and quaysides to whole nights around a table with friends. (At the end of his life Gide complained in his curmudgeonly way that conversations generally bored him and wore him out, except with a precious few. He feared and fled them, he said, but I don't quite believe him. Perhaps his weariness was just part of his loss of appetite for life towards the end.)

There were all those friendships of his as well, constellations of friendships, pulsing, brightening, dying away... No, there was no need for words on the slab at our feet. It had all been said—'more or less well', as he once observed himself—although by no means only by André Gide.

'Have you noticed?' Zaïda was smiling. 'These geraniums are real, they're fresh.' And so they were. The red geraniums on both graves were the only fresh flowers in the whole cemetery. Somebody's memory of them was still alive and precious. I think André would have agreed that ordinary red geraniums struck just the right note.

♦

'You know, I feel really sorry for Madeleine,' Miriam said as we drove off, winding through the streets of this closed-off little town. 'What a miserable life she had.'

'Well, at least she was miserable in comfort,' Zaïda said. 'Left or right here?'

'Left, obviously,' I said. 'I do and I don't feel sorry for her. At least they loved each other—and deeply, too, all their lives, although it sometimes didn't look like it. It's just that each of them wanted to love somebody the other couldn't be. He couldn't be a virtuous husband—it wasn't in his repertoire—and she couldn't be an angel.' I was about to expand on 'angel', but this wasn't the right moment. We now seemed to be rocketing towards Le

Havre, when we should've been pointing in the other direction, towards Rouen. Besides, I wasn't sure that the mention of hyperpresences would cut much ice with these two. 'Hasn't that ever happened to you?'

'No,' said Miriam, 'I can't say that it has.'

'Well, it's happened to me.'

'And it's happened to me, too,' said Zaïda, trying to read a road sign as we flashed past. 'Twice since Christmas, as a matter of fact.'

'He tried not to love her, and she tried to make herself as unlovable as possible, turning herself into some kind of pious drudge, supervising the housekeeping, feeding crippled dogs and reading nothing but the *Imitation of Christ*, but he loved her utterly. When she died he lost his appetite for living and never got it back, really. He lost his axis, as he put it, the one fixed point in his existence. She was his reality. Without her he only pretended to be alive.'

'And was he her "reality"?'

'No, God was. She spent her whole life repaying God for her mother's sin.'

'Poor Madeleine.' Miriam had no time for this kind of delusion. 'It's like agoraphobia,' she used to say about any kind of god delusion. 'Irrational, but reason alone can't cure it.'

'But she did love him.' I wanted her to know this. 'She judged him and found him wanting, as she judged all sinners, but she did love him.'

'She wasn't the only one, it seems.'

I wasn't going to bite. After a brief Chekhovian pause, I said, 'It depends on what you mean by "love".' It didn't, to be honest. Whatever you meant by it, Madeleine wasn't the only one to love him. They loved him from afar, both men and women, sometimes passionately; they loved him as a master (schoolboys, having read *Fruits of the Earth*, would throw themselves into his arms in the street); and they loved him as a friend who, in Roger Martin du Gard's words, never failed to enrich them, even if they only met for an hour and he was at his most tyrannical and self-obsessed; they loved him as a family member, whatever he might have written about families (the Allégrets, the Van Rysselberghes). It was such a tangled web of loves that I thought I might get snarled in it if I started to explain, especially about Elisabeth Van Rysselberghe, who had borne his child. This just wasn't the moment, especially for mentioning Elisabeth.

It was tempting, though. They'd be agog, naturally. Elisabeth Van Rysselberghe had been Marc's lover at one time, as well as Rupert Brooke's, but had her child, not by Rupert or Marc, but by none other than Marc's erstwhile lover, André Gide. It was a daughter, Catherine, conceived during a Sunday morning stroll by the sea at Hyères-Plage, a stroll during which, in Elisabeth's mother Maria Van Rysselberghe's words, he rediscovered the complete freedom with which amorous dispositions are favoured. Very nicely put. Very *Fruits of the Earth*.

The coupling on the beach in 1922 was not quite as inadvertent as it might seem. Fifteen years earlier in Rome his friend and now 'mother-in-law' Maria had sensed some sort of simmering mutual attraction between Elisabeth and Gide—something 'more than friendship and interest'—and in 1916, in the corridor of a train they were returning to Paris on, he had passed her an extraordinary note: 'I shall only ever truly *love* one woman and I can only have real desires for boys. But I find it hard to resign myself to seeing you childless and to having no child of my own.' Now, that's a note to give a young woman pause for thought.

When told of Elisabeth's pregnancy, Gide was apparently 'vertiginous' with joy—'drunk and at the same time thrown off balance'. Indeed, everyone seems to have felt vertiginous, except for Madeleine, who didn't know about it. Gide became by all accounts a devoted, if clandestine, father.

Then there was Marc Allégret himself. 'If you mean Marc Allégret...'

'Was that *the* Marc Allégret, by the way, the film director?'

'Yes.'

'Beuzeville!' Zaïda cried suddenly, having slowed down sufficiently to read a road sign. 'Let's go to Beuzeville! With a name like that, how could we not?

We'll find a nice café somewhere and have a good *beuze*.' It's as senseless in French as it is in English, but sounds vaguely like something you might like to do together once the children have gone off to bed.

'Yes, why not?' said Miriam, who was starting to look a bit rattled by the hit-or-miss way we were progressing. 'And you can tell us more about the affair with Marc Allégret. I'm curious.'

'Oh, it's a very long story.' 'Well, give us the short version.' 'How short?'

'The one-teapot version.'

And so, over tea and *palmiers* in a patisserie in Beuzeville, just down the road from Beuzeville railway station from which Gide used to set off for St Lazare and his rendezvous with Marc Allégret, I recounted, to an attentive, but not uncritical, audience:

The Beuzeville Version of the Marc Allégret Story or 'The Ideal Friend'

It was a *coup de foudre*. Not 'love at first sight', because Gide had known Marc ever since he was born—Marc was the fourth child of the man who had witnessed his wedding—but precisely a *coup de foudre*, a lightning bolt. But not even lightning strikes out of an empty sky. (Zaïda said that that just showed how much I knew about *coups de foudre*, but I let that pass.) And the sky in May 1917 was particularly turbulent. I don't mean the war—the clouds of war were roiling blackly well away towards the horizon to the north and east—I mean the sky directly above André Gide's head. The year before, Madeleine had opened a letter to her husband from his old partner in crime Henri Ghéon, who was at the front. Ghéon had converted to Catholicism, along with a whole string of other friends of his: when European civilisation seems about to collapse, a certain kind of person does. Ghéon was probably writing to urge his old comrade in debauchery to mend his ways.

('What do you think the attraction of Catholicism is for homosexuals?' Miriam interjected, snapping off a bit of sugary *palmier* and popping it into her mouth. 'I mean, it can't be just the frocks.' 'No, not just that. I think it's more that in the Catholic Church it's easier to find your own level, if you know what I mean. For Protestants there are no levels. There's the Truth, which is implacable, and there's you—that's it—whereas the Catholic Church is very placable indeed. That was Luther's whole point, wasn't it?' Miriam looked unconvinced.)

Anyway, there it was at last, in black and white: a description of what her husband got up to on certain boulevards in Paris, in the bathhouses, in North Africa, where he'd travelled with Ghéon—and it wasn't just a matter of stroking some schoolboy's downy arm through a train window. You can forget the tent scene in *Brokeback Mountain*, though. Gide's encounters were always much more ... (It was difficult to find words suitable for afternoon tea in a provincial patisserie. Miriam suggested 'adolescent', which was too demure, but then Zaïda came up with 'He liked to have a grope') . . . a matter of ecstatic groping. He doesn't seem to have wanted to possess anybody, or be possessed, if you know what I mean. Yes, he was greedy, but not for possession. All the same, for a woman who probably thought Jane Austen was racy, reading that letter must have been a profound shock.

Some have suggested that what Madeleine got her hands on while her husband was away in Paris was not Ghéon's letter but scraps of her husband's own writing, which he was in the habit of leaving all over the house, wherever he'd sat to scribble something down. It could've been anything, really—notes, a draft for one of his books, diary entries he later destroyed—but, whatever it was, it was clearly devastating. A detailed image of her husband's double. Their marriage seems to have now become a cold desert, with Madeleine retreating even further into household chores and nun-like devoutness and Gide sinking into lethargy, his thoughts occupied with nothing but growing old (he wasn't yet fifty) and death. He was ripe for a last throw of the dice.

As often as he could, he got away, naturally, and when he was in Paris he saw a lot of his old friend Elie Allégret's family, even staying with them sometimes. Now, Elie, who was by this time a pastor, went off to the Cameroons in early 1917 to work with the Protestant missions there, asking André, who had once been his pupil, to keep an eye on his family—he'd left his wife, three young sons and a daughter at home. That's really what I meant when I said that even lightning doesn't strike out of an empty sky: the Devil himself couldn't have come up with a more cunning plan of seduction. A stagnant, sexless marriage in Cuverville and here in Paris a rebellious seventeen-year-old boy needing a father, a teacher, a guide—needing love from an older man. I mean, this lightning bolt was practically preordained.

Now, as we all know, to look at somebody and think to yourself 'Dishy!' doesn't of itself produce a *coup de foudre*. That happens to all of us several times a day—well, to me, at any rate, especially in the Paris metro—but there's no bolt of lightning. There might even be a fluttering of the emotions, the heart might go sickeningly *boom*, but a genuine *coup de foudre* is something else entirely. (For a moment or two we all sat in silence, casting our minds back.) Marc was undeniably good-looking in precisely the way Gide found irresistible—dark-haired, graceful with just a touch of the urchin, tenderly boisterous, grown-up but still gamin, a gaily coloured kite, as I might say, begging to be reeled in. I must show you a photograph when we get back. There was nothing of the effete brat about him—Gide's and Wilde's tastes were very different. But there were good-looking youths on every street corner in Paris, after all, yet Gide didn't fall in love with them. For that to happen a bolt of electricity has to pass between you—or you have to believe it did—a look, a gesture, or, best of all, a smile. Gide himself put it very well, I think: his desires, he said, responded to a certain *gourmandise* in the other—greediness, appetite, what's the right word? Without that all you're left with is a crush. This was no mere crush. In any case, Gide didn't really go in for one-sided crushes. He even claimed that that was the secret of his happiness. And young Marc Allégret at this moment, Gide tells us, was '*toute gourmandise sensuelle*'—'all sensual gluttony'.

In short, at some point in the spring or early summer of 1917, while he was staying with the Allégrets in Paris, zap! He and the boy he'd known since birth, scarcely noticing him, became a couple. Their letters to each other from those first years are dizzying to read. Gide was giddy with happiness. Marc in his overwrought, adolescent way was almost frantic with greedy excitement. And for Gide this love he'd found, he told his diary when it first began, was the only thing occupying his mind and flesh.

At this point Miriam put the teapot down rather sharply. 'So while millions were dying in the mud all over Europe, all the great man could think about was his infatuation with some teenaged boy.'

'I think you're being unfair. In the first place, he worked tirelessly with refugees during the war, he was assistant head of the Foyer Franco-Belge; and in the second place, the fact that the world is awash with suffering doesn't mean that *you* have no right to happiness. Do you imagine that nobody fell in love during the plague, for instance, or wept over a lost love during the siege of Leningrad? Anyway, my whole point is that it wasn't something he willed to happen—it just happened, like an asteroid slamming into the earth. There's a wonderful essay of Lytton Strachey's, actually—have you read it?—with a title that's just the date of some Monday in 1916, in which all he does is ramble on about how "extraordinarily happy" he is, about inconsequential arguments with Duncan and Vanessa and lusting after the postman as well as some boxer whose photograph he's come across in that morning's newspaper—he was quite besotted with this boxer, even fantasised about taking him to Garsington Manor to lunch—and kissing David Garnett in the garden and getting quite excited about it. It's an essay about nothing, really, trivialities. Meanwhile, just across the Channel...'

Miriam looked anything but mollified. 'So what? All that proves is that Lytton Strachey was as self-obsessed as Gide was.' She ordered a second pot of tea.

Marc began writing his 'Uncle André' the most outrageously affectionate letters, calling himself *'ton petit Marc'*, assuring him of his tender love (*'je t'aime de toute ma tendresse'*)—telling him how badly he missed him and needed him, how he wanted nothing more than to see him again from the moment he said goodbye, ending a rambling letter about his school-work and the day's adventures by kissing his uncle 'voluptuously' or even 'breathing in his smell'. ('He's starting to sound positively sluttish,' Miriam murmured, gobbling down more *palmier*.) Once he said he'd 'howled' with excitement when he'd seen his uncle's handwriting on an envelope.

André's letters back were much more restrained. Full of suppressed emotion, naturally, but usually adopting the tone of the loving teacher, dispensing advice to his sometimes rather feckless pupil about what to read, how to behave, how to soar above mediocrity. They were solicitous letters, even severely admonishing letters, although he did once admit that he had to hold back from saying 'stupid things', unsuitable things, despite the fact that they were certainly whirling around wildly in his head—and heart.

Marc was not homosexual. In later life far from it— he had several wives and many lovers, even while married. Yes, this love was between two men, but all Marc was doing at the beginning was living out the advice his 'uncle' had offered in *Fruits of the Earth* to his fictional young friend Nathaniël. Marc was being Nathaniël in the flesh, craving to leave his family and unlearn all he'd been taught, just as his 'uncle' had once written that a young man should. At the same time as he was being uprooted, though, made 'homeless', if you like— and this is important—he was being rooted in French cultural life: told what to read, fed ideas. He was being his teacher's ideal pupil. More than that, he was being the adolescent Gide wished he could have been himself, had he not been bound hand and foot—swaddled, really, tightly bandaged—in religious dogma. He was being his uncle's ideal double at an age when Gide himself had still been taking cold baths, sleeping on a hard board and rising in the middle of the night to say his prayers.

Now, it's a cliché, I know, but nonetheless true: just days after falling in love you start to hatch a plan to have your beloved all to yourself. There he is, all tangled up in attachments to family and friends, his attention darting from brothers to pals to obligations of no real interest to you (although you always feign intense interest at first)—family outings, his football club, movies he's just seen, his passion for some pop-star or cause. You have to take him away from all this. A weekend by the sea, a trip somewhere exotic—it doesn't matter where you go or for how long, but all those tiresome ties he keeps chattering on about need slicing through before they strangle both of you. He needs to be taken somewhere remote from all that where you can start remoulding him, opening his eyes to how big the world is. Nowhere too exciting at first, naturally, because then it might strike him how ordinary you really are. Strachey, by the way, fantasised (quite unsuitably) about taking the boxer whose half-naked picture he'd seen in the paper that morning to Garsington Manor (of all places) for the weekend to meet Lady Ottoline Morrell and the rest of the tribe. The mere thought of it made him so dazzlingly happy that it felt like a religious conversion. 'June 26th 1916', that's the name of the essay, it's just come to me. I wonder what was happening on the Eastern Front *that* day.

Anyway, Gide settled on England as the place to whisk Marc off to—Cambridge, to be precise. Where, Gide being Gide, in the summer of 1918 they met none other than Lytton Strachey, not to mention a host of other stars in the English intellectual firmament—Housman, Maynard Keynes, Roger Fry, I can't remember them all off the top of my head—and Strachey's sister Dorothy fell in love with him—with André, I mean, not young Marc. I think she probably mistook her fall for a *coup de foudre*, but it wasn't. It was a one-sided instant infatuation, not the same thing at all.

I can see you think England an odd choice. Why not Florence or Algiers? Well, the excuse for the trip was that Gide would chaperone Marc while he learnt English, but for the humble pastor's son from Paris it must have been a dizzying experience: not just mixing with people like Diaghilev, Aldous Huxley and Lady Ottoline Morrell (speaking of Garsington Manor), but going to the opera, the ballet, art galleries, fashionable dinners in grand houses ... it must have been life-changing. Marc stayed on in England for a while after André went home and even joined the Royal Flying Corps, so in a sense grew up while he was there. He arrived as a boy, if you like, and left a man.

It was when Gide got back to Cuverville that things went seriously awry. Not with Marc, but with Madeleine. The night before he left for England Madeleine had made it clear in her off-putting see-nothing, hear-nothing way that she knew perfectly well what was going on: she was being abandoned by her husband at Cuverville, with the Germans just outside Paris, while he popped off to England with his male lover. She didn't put it like that, naturally. She just asked him if he was going with Marc and then, before he could say a word, cut him off. 'Don't say anything,' she said. 'Never tell me anything again. I prefer your silence to your deceit.' Something like that. It was so like her—so like a hyperpresence. You can't *argue* with a tutelary deity. But he wasn't deceiving her, he just wasn't spelling it out. Later that night he wrote her a letter, telling her that he felt he was dying at Cuverville, rotting away, becoming a corpse, and that he wanted to live, and this meant travelling, meeting people, loving people. As the Immoralist said of his wife, Madeleine was giving rest to a man who wasn't tired. That may sound kind, but it's lethal.

First thing next morning he gave her the letter—*and*

she wrote back! While her husband was preparing to leave for the station, she wrote back. If only she could've said it to him, knocked on his door, come into his room and said it to him. It was a beautiful letter, the sort that, once read, you never quite forget. She says that he's free, has always been free, to come and go as he wishes. She even says that she knows he loves her, and that she loves him. What distresses her is his sinful way of life—there, she's put it in writing. It will lead him to perdition. She tells him to resist. Why would he? By now he has no strong belief in either sin or perdition.

Gide once wrote that there was no weapon that didn't lose its edge against Madeleine's gentleness, her *douceur*. Everything simply slid off her. She didn't jib at anything, didn't protest, just bent like a reed in the wind and then, once the wind died down, stood up straight again, convinced of her own uprightness. Well, this letter illustrates this side to Madeleine's character perfectly.

It was while he was in England that this gentle reed showed her true force of character. She took all his letters to her, reread them one by one and then burnt them. It took days. All of them, even those he wrote to her as a boy. It was like the ritual murder of . . . I'm not sure what . . . something beautiful their love for each other had given birth to, it was as if she were killing their only child. And, if that sounds melodramatic, it's what he said. When he found out what she'd done—by accident, by the way, he just wanted to check something in one of his old letters and she went pale and told him that she'd burnt them—he was devastated, grief-stricken. 'Why did you do it?' he wept. 'Can't you see that you've destroyed the best part of me?' 'I was suffering too much,' Madeleine replied, with infinite composure, I imagine, 'I had to do something... *they were what was most precious to me.*' To her.

He wept for a week, he says. In fact, he says that in a way he never recovered from the savage blow of having those letters destroyed, never quite regained his taste for life, never felt *real* again.

('I know what he means,' Zaïda said. 'When someone close to you dies, that's exactly how you feel—unreal.' 'But not for the rest of your life,' Miriam snapped. 'In my opinion, he had it coming. To tell you the truth, I'm surprised she didn't burn the whole house down. Let's go, shall we?')

♦

As we drove out of Beuzeville in the pinkish-grey of the late afternoon, nobody spoke for a while. Then Zaïda, who has a weakness for catastrophic endings—not a comfort when you're changing lanes on the A29 with semi-trailers from Bulgaria hurtling past like jumbo jets—said: 'So how did it end?'

'Well, they lived on at Cuverville for another twenty

years or so in silence, with Madeleine behaving more and more like the member of some mendicant order—paying off her mother's debt to God, and André darting off to Paris, Berlin, the Congo, Moscow...'

'No, I mean the affair with Marc Allégret.'

'Well, in a sort of a way it didn't end. That's one of the most touching things about it. They travelled together, they even lived together in Paris at different times, and as Marc grew up they slowly became profoundly affectionate friends. More than affectionate: it was a bond of love that was never broken. Somehow or other, Gide managed to turn a great passion into a great friendship, and that's rarer than it sounds. Marc was at his bedside when he breathed his last. Some might even say—some have said—that the reason Marc never found his perfect companion in a woman (and believe me, he tried) is that nobody, man or woman, could match his *cher petit oncle*, André Gide, his accomplice, his protector, his teacher and his most intimate friend. Gide was in a very real sense everything to him. How many of us can say we've been that to anybody?'

'Some day,' said Zaïda after a pause, 'I must read the long version of this story. I'm sure you've left a lot of vital things out.'

Miriam didn't say anything, but I had the distinct impression we'd soon be having one of our frank conversations, this time about the right to happiness in a wretched world, perhaps, or how I'd had the wool pulled over my eyes by this wily Frenchman. They're immensely bracing, these conversations of ours. A spark flies—just a syllable or two sometimes: about the pope, for example, or whether or not money can buy happiness (it obviously can, but usually doesn't)—and before you know it there's a brushfire scooting off in all directions. Miriam has a gift for raillery (when she walks, as it were, you hear the sharp click of her heels) and without that any conversation is just talk. But not tonight. Tonight we were all too sunk in our own thoughts to even sing. At St Lazare, where they dropped me off, the African men with the drums and xylophone were making the corridors reverberate again with their agitated rhythms. Africa. 'Bare feet on blue tiles.' I was ready for Africa.

7.

SOUSSE

In the rue Souk El Caïd that morning absolutely nothing was happening. From time to time a pink English couple in shorts and sun-hats would traipse past towards the covered markets at the bottom of the hill, obliging the bored young souvenir-sellers lounging outside their stalls to make a half-hearted attempt to interest them in a brass plate or stuffed camel, but nobody was buying. 'Madame, monsieur, come inside, *venez, entrez, kommen Sie herein*... I have many beautiful plates, handmade in Sousse, *sehr schön* ...' But with a wave of a pink hand they would plod past, stunned by the heat, although it was only late March.

At one point a clutch of elderly Germans picked its way up the stepped street—you could hear the ripple of coaxing calls following them uphill—but they too swatted the young men aside and kept grimly climbing. On their way to the casbah, probably, the old citadel on the edge of the medina just above us. A museum now, full of fabulous Roman mosaics, it's the only thing worth seeing in Sousse, at least from an elderly German point of view, the only real *Sehnswürdigkeit*.

'Auf Wiedersehen . . .' the boy opposite me called after them in a trailing voice. He wouldn't be seeing them again, though. And knew it and didn't care. He leant back against the whitewashed wall in the shade and flashed me a grin. '*Ça va?*' He didn't care about that, either, clearly, but polite banter was his job.

As it happened, things couldn't have been better. After the noisy chaos of Tunis, this tranquil corner of Sousse was bliss. For a start, I love places where there's nothing much to see in the way of *Sehnswürdigkeiten* (there's no real English equivalent: 'things sightseers should see'). *Sehnswürdigkeiten*—cathedrals, palaces, national museums, monuments, anything remotely military—make me tense. I'd just spent an arduous day up in Carthage trudging around the ruins, yapped at by guides and fried in the sun. Punic houses, Roman villas, a museum, an amphitheatre, baths, basilicas, a necropolis . . . and that was only scratching the surface. In Sousse there's absolutely nothing at all you *have* to see, once you've admired the Roman mosaics displayed in the casbah. You're free. Now you can start looking. Would Yacoub have understood this? Perhaps not. He's one of those people, I think, who never stop collecting the pieces for life's great jigsaw. He seems to be persuaded that it's all going to add up to something. Zaïda goes to the other extreme: she claims to have spent a whole week in Athens without bothering to climb up to the Parthenon. I myself once visited Cairo and missed the pyramids.

However, as Gide once said, to free yourself is nothing—it's being free that's hard. 'It's when I'm freest that I feel the furthest from happiness,' he once wrote ruefully in one of his purposeful, Protestant moods. Nietzsche also thought that being free was difficult, but usefully so: it sorted the sheep from the goats. 'The man who has become free,' he wrote, 'spurns the contemptible sort of well-being dreamed of by shop-keepers, Christians, cows, women, Englishmen and other democrats. The free man is a warrior . . .' Not many warriors in the rue Souk El Caïd that morning. More to the point, the passers-by seemed without exception to be shopkeepers, Christians, women, Englishmen and other democrats (no cows), mostly at a complete loss to know what to do with their freedom, but vaguely aware that they should be doing *something*. By the look on their faces most of those plodding past me (I was sitting under an umbrella drinking a freshly squeezed orange juice) were still doing what Gide would call 'rowing', or at least going through the motions. On the very eve of sailing for North Africa he wrote in his diary that he was 'like a sailor who drops his oars and abandons himself to the currents; at last he takes the time to look at the shores; as long as he was rowing he didn't look'.

Under my umbrella I was leafing through a book I'd found on old Sousse—*A la recherche du Sousse d'antan*, it was called (*In Search of the Sousse of Yesteryear*). Although my eye was partly on what was happening around me—the strolling cats, the drifts of tourists (all that bare flesh, a shock in these surroundings) and the svelte young man across from me, vainly trying to lure them into his shop—my mind was in a yesteryear sort of mood. Not nostalgic (I'd never experienced old Sousse) but tinged with a sort of regretfulness that I hadn't.

In the book there happened to be a painting of the very street I was sitting in. It dated from about the time the French first arrived there in 1891—just before young André got there, exhausted after four days' travel in a landau from Tunis with his friend Paul Laurens (but without his Bible). The walls in the painting are a yellowish-white, the street is made of dirt, and there are lots of turbaned men in short blue and brown garments making their way up the hill on their basket-laden donkeys or squatting in the shade talking. In those days the street was apparently known for its saddle-makers and woodworkers; in all the laneways branching off it they made ladders, ploughs, olive-picking hooks, and so on from the wood of olive trees. On a warm morning like this one, if André and Paul had passed this way, they would have been assailed by the smell of leather, sawdust and donkey-dung, and they'd probably have caught a whiff of freshly dyed wool as well from further up the hill where the weavers worked, not to mention the stench from the open drains. On this particular morning I couldn't really smell anything at all—just a hint of frying fish, perhaps. And all the men were wearing jeans. As in the painting, there were no women.

In point of fact, by the time André and Paul reached Sousse, winter was closing in. In addition, André's health was so precarious by this time, with only one lung functioning and a worrying fever, that I doubt he could have climbed as steep a street as the Souk El Caïd even if he'd wanted to. When he wasn't resting at his inn, he probably stuck to the lively laneways around the Great Mosque, venturing occasionally as far as the sleepy port underneath the medina's eastern wall. In those days, not long after the French had established their Protectorate, Sousse was no more than a village—a *bourgade*, as the French called it—just a few thousand Arabs, Berbers and Jews, with a sprinkling of Sicilians and Maltese, mostly squashed inside the medina by the silted-up harbour where I was now enjoying my orange juice. Although he says little about it (he was feeling too tubercular to take much interest), we know from photographs and paintings precisely what he'd have seen in the medina: a walled maze of narrow alleyways, some bursting into life as bazaars soon after daybreak, as they still do today, each at that time with its own specialty. In this laneway sat the tailors, swatting at flies, over there were wool-merchants surrounded by piles of greasy fleeces, around the corner fruit and vegetable sellers, while across the tiny square past the fountain there'd have been jewellers and cobblers, many of them (as they do today) working at their craft in small rooms opening straight onto the street. He'd have found a perfume-seller, too, before long, I should think, sitting in his closet-like shop—André loved buying perfume in those slim glass vials with wax stoppers. Jasmine, geranium and damask rose oil, essence of orange blossom, aromatic candles—it's hard to walk past a perfume-seller's booth without feeling that you've started to float. And on the street, dodging the *karatonis* (the two-wheeled carts pulled by a mule or horse) they would have seen only men and boys, mostly in burnouses as the days grew colder. André and Paul had gone native in Tunis as soon as they'd arrived there a few weeks earlier, but here in Sousse, with winter closing in, they'd resorted to their usual overcoats and shawls. You can still time-travel in Sousse if you dare.

For all the electric lights in the stalls, the television screens in the tea-houses, the young men in jeans and lurid T-shirts, the bare-headed Arab girls drinking cappuccinos in the sun and the hordes of tourists from countries the locals had never heard of in Gide's day, inside the walls of the medina you can still catch yourself dreaming that you've been catapulted back several centuries. Five minutes' walk away, outside the walls in the European quarter by the sea, you could be anywhere—Mexico, Portugal, Australia—it's twenty-first-century vacation land. There along the beachfront, as along countless beachfronts all over the world, stretch high-rise hotels, restaurants, bars and cafés; tourists from every continent wander up and down in a daze, waiting for something to happen—to feel thirsty, see a donkey, be accosted, anything. But in the medina your imagination can still take flight, if you'll let it.

I wondered that day in the Souk El Caïd if Gide's imagination might not have swooped back more than several centuries. The night before in my hotel room I'd been reading one of those highly entertaining detective novels set in Ancient Rome that you can buy at any airport bookstall these days. If only we'd had them when I did Roman history at school—they make it so much easier to remember who Vespasian was, for instance, or what the Romans were doing in Gaul. As I plunged back into the description of Pompeii and Herculaneum in AD 71, just before Vesuvius buried them in lava and ash, picturing the brothels, the bakers' shops and the fast-food bars on many street corners, the market squares, the temples and so on, I was struck by how similar it all was to the medinas in Tunisia in modern times. In the narrow streets, lined with the same lock-up booths selling the same wares, there would have been the same donkey-carts, the same jostling crowds of shoppers, some attired like royalty, some barely managing to stay alive. No wine, of course, in North African souks, but olives, sunflower seeds, spices, fish, raw meat, gherkins, lettuces and eggs just as there were in Pompeii and Herculaneum. And men playing draughts, although the bawdy-houses these days are well-hidden in North Africa, which they certainly weren't on the Bay of Naples. Even in the houses, which were closed off to the street, revealing nothing of the elegance inside, there was the same profusion of perfume jars, oil flasks, sandalwood boxes for jewellery and combs, mirrors, coffers for clothes, and the same inner courtyard, usually with a pool or fountain. It struck me, in other words, that part of the allure of North Africa for the young Gide with Virgil in his pocket must have been the sensation of being transported back into a world he was half in love with. Tunis was Roman antiquity brought to life, yet magically he could buy a ticket there on the boat.

For me, though, it's not so much what I see when I wake in the morning and look down from my hotel window that hurls me back centuries in a town like Sousse—the tangle of blue and white streets, seething with swarthy figures, some in long robes and turbaned. It's not even the sounds and smells washing over me as soon as I enter one of the laneways in the souk—the wailing music, the roosters crowing, the hammers on copper, the pools of tangy aromas lying in the cool at shop doorways. It has more to do with the way people approach and talk to one another, look at one another, sit with each other, touch one another. I mean the men—women pass by like characters from a different novel, one you're not allowed to read. To watch these men is like letting your eyes rest on an ancient carpet, densely woven, intricately patterned, mostly indecipherable and, miraculously, despite centuries of wear, still glowing brightly as if fresh from the loom.

After days in the medina I still can't work out what the patterns on this carpet mean. Yes, this is a rose, this a camel's foot and this seems to be a fountain, but what does it all mean? I don't understand what is shameful and what is perfectly good manners here, what is forbidden and what is harmless play, what is deference and what is gentle mockery. I don't know, in short, what it means to be a man here, dealing with other men.

Sometimes, opening my mouth to speak, I hear a voice I barely recognise saying things I'd only imagined myself saying before. In the flurry of teasing exchanges that accompany me up the street, who is courting whom? Who, in the terms of Ottoman courtship ritual, is the 'lover' and who the prospective 'beloved'? Or am I indeed just a man buying an ice-cream? Further along the street, for just a fraction of a second, I feel I should be plying this gazelle-eyed youth, who has taken me by the elbow to entice me into buying one of his finely sewn djellabas, with a many-versed *ghazel* about perfumed gardens and nightingales. But my Mastercard will probably do. One thing is reasonably certain, though: whoever is courting whom, I am the one about to be duped.

◆

On my third morning in Sousse I felt a surge of restlessness. I needed something to spark my flagging appetite for the coming day. As Miriam says, it's the third morning that is always the most fragile because by then you've drifted back down to earth, remembering, with a touch of disenchantment and a sense of growing 'clutter', as she puts it with a flicker of irritation, exactly who you're supposed to be. Something Roman would do nicely at this point, I thought to myself, something gracefully severe to offset the chaos of the medina, something measured, verging on silence, in counterpoint to the cacophony outside my window. El Jem has one of the largest and most magnificent amphitheatres in the world. El Jem, only an hour's dash in a minibus across the plain from Sousse, could be just the ticket.

In *The Immoralist* Gide's protagonist Michel finds El Jem disappointing and even 'ugly', but he was tired and ill at the time. All the same, I can see that you have to be in the right mood for El Jem—a Johann Wolfgang von Goethe sort of mood, perhaps. When Goethe reached Assisi on his way to Rome, he astounded and profoundly irked the locals by 'turning away with distaste' from the towering glories of the Basilica of St Francis. Who did this German fop think he was? Instead of admiring Giotto's frescoes on the life of St Francis, or the high, light-filled nave of the Upper Basilica, for instance, or in the Lower Basilica Cimabue's 'Madonna with Four Angels and St Francis', or the rose window or the cloisters of transporting beauty, instead of even just standing back and basking in the overwhelming grandeur of this vast monument to Catholic myth-making, as even the most scatterbrained tourist might do, the bumptious author of *The Sorrows of Young Werther* and minister of state at the time in some minor German duchy fixed his attention on the Temple of Minerva some distance away in the heart of the medieval town. Even today it only gets one star in my Michelin guide: in other words, hardly worth going out of your way for. Not only that, Goethe also announced that this ancient Roman temple aroused in him indescribable sensations, which he knew would stay with him forever.

I find this story heartening. Now, it's true that Goethe was also moved to spend only three hours of his two years in Italy on Florence, which was eccentric of him to say the least. For that matter, he barely noticed St Mark's Basilica in Venice—or the Doges' Palace—and couldn't be bothered with trying to find Juliet's balcony in Verona. This is arguably not just eccentric but practically perverse. All the same, I find the Assisi story exhilarating. At thirty-seven, on his first trip to Italy, Goethe was already a true traveller.

It's not that I don't regard the Basilica in Assisi as worth visiting if you feel so inclined, it's just that I admire travellers who refuse to be stampeded into gazing at things they don't believe will enrich them... I was about to say 'spiritually', but that's a word best avoided ... things that won't *thicken* their experience of being alive. Just because everyone else feels obliged to climb the Eiffel Tower or mill around gawking in St Peter's in Rome doesn't mean that we should. Goethe was no bystander at some street carnival, as so many of us are when we travel. For whatever reason, he did not feel *thickened* by the medieval, or even by the Renaissance, so the St Francis saga didn't enliven him. He wasn't much interested in the Gothic, either, for that matter, all those 'spiky little towers and cast-iron flowers'. What he was instinctively drawn to once he'd arrived in Italy was the expression of balance and proportion he found in all its restrained sensuousness in the monuments from classical antiquity. And his instincts were right: what he found at the Temple of Minerva, even if it was by this time St Mary's Church Above Minerva (one goddess of wisdom having replaced the other), was one of the best preserved Roman façades in all Italy: six Corinthian columns crowned by a pediment, with a high door in the portico leading into the sacred interior. It was pagan, harmonious, frozen yet dynamic, and it struck at Goethe's quick, changing the way he thought and wrote. That's at the heart of why we travel.

The colosseum looms above the ugly jumble of the modern town of El Jem like a sinister mirage. When I first caught sight of it, unexpectedly, turning a corner near the bus-station, I just stood there staring at it, stunned. It could hardly be real, it was so out of scale, so astonishingly intact and quite deserted, as if I'd conjured it up in a trance. Three curving tiers of open galleries in yellow limestone, all empty at that hour in the morning. Grace and power—and as well as slaughter on a grand, almost voluptuous, scale—all rising out of an ancient sea of olive oil. Olives were the petroleum of this part of Africa in Roman times.

Once inside, though, with my guide striding out ahead of me, directing a stream of information at me over her shoulder in rapid-fire French, the trance melted away. Phoenicians, Romans, emperors, proconsuls, revolts, sieges, Arab conquerors, wars... I couldn't take it all in, I couldn't anchor it all in any grid of stories lying deep inside me. Corinthian columns, Doric columns, pilasters, voussoirs and archivolts—it all began to blur. Even down in the stone cells beneath the arena, where gladiators once waited for their turn to die, I found it difficult to connect what I was seeing and hearing with any living web of thought or experience inside me. It was all fascinating information, but it wouldn't stick. From the top row in the arena, the view was breathtaking, I could just begin to picture (if I blocked out the chatter of the guide) the tens of thousands of spectators, roaring with excitement at the carnage taking place below them. There would have been sweet-sellers, drink-sellers, wine merchants, perfume-sellers, prostitutes, pickpockets and dribs and drabs of people dashing in late, arrayed in all their finery ... But no, even then the vision faded quickly away, sliding past me, as it were, leaving few traces ... and my mind turned to lunch. It was a Goethean moment, I suppose, although he might well have found this Roman arena embedding itself in very fertile ground indeed inside him. I didn't think of Goethe, though, until I was finishing my lunch.

I was in one of those slightly down-at-heel cafés lining the promenade opposite the arena, eating a cheese sandwich while gazing back (rather vacantly, I must admit) at the arcaded wonder just across from me. I was the only customer. The young waiter was sitting on a table under the awning with a friend, idly swinging his legs and trying from time to time to catch my attention. '*Ça va?*' he called. (Well, that could mean anything.)

'*Oui, merci, ça va.*' I took a sip of tepid coffee. '*Tu es seul?*' Here we go, I thought. Where is your wife? Where is your friend? Why are you alone? Would you like me to be your friend?

'*Oui, tout seul.*'

Then he surprised me: '*Tu es content?*'

'Content?'

'*Content, heureux.*' He wanted to know if I was happy.

'Do you mean at this moment or in life in general?'

He and his friend both smiled. 'I mean, are you a happy man?'

'Yes,' I said, 'I think I am. Are you?'

'Yes, very happy. All you need to be happy is work, girls and a glass of beer. Don't you agree?' Legs still swinging, boyish grin.

Now, this was a moment well worth coming to El Jem for. I felt a tiny detonation of warm pleasure deep inside. But how should I answer? *'Jusqu'à un certain point,'* I said. And 'up to a point' I did agree: it's the ancient ideal of the simple, but satisfying, life. It's the life Virgil's shepherd lads dreamt of, it's more or less what Goethe believed peasant boys thought of as the 'good life'—good bread, good beer and good soup. In other words, work followed by the nourishment and pleasure that love assures you of. Needless to say, it's not nearly enough—not for Virgil or Goethe or even for me. What makes me happy (but how could I have explained this to the waiter?) is being interrupted while eating a sandwich in front of one of the Roman empire's greatest architectural triumphs by the waiter telling me what he thinks happiness is. Just like the façade of the Temple of Minerva, this cut straight to my quick because it was both big and little at the same time or, as Gide deftly put it when writing about Goethe, it was banality of a superior kind. I was elated. I set off for the museum across town with a new spring in my step.

Walking back to my hotel in Sousse that evening, slightly dazed by all the mosaics in the museum at El Jem and the hair-raising dash in the oven-like heat back to the coast, I felt pleasantly *thickened* by the day—not deepened, but nourished and fortified. Rounding the corner of the Great Mosque (more a fortress than a mosque: an immense open courtyard surrounded by massive stone walls) I caught myself wondering why Gide had not shown more interest in Islam. After all, Islam is so Protestant, at least compared to Catholicism, and at the same time, in practice, so able to accommodate a whole variety of loves in the gentle drift towards the love of God. It might be interesting, I thought, to pop over to Kairouan in the morning, in Kairouan there were mosques Gide was drawn to.

In the hotel foyer the Tennessee Baptists were assembling for dinner. 'Good evening!' I murmured, smiling guardedly.

'Good evening!' they chorused, beaming. 'The Lord reigns!' Not, as I was to discover, in Kairouan, He didn't.

It was here in Sousse, however, more or less where the high-rise hotels stretch out forlornly now along the seafront, that the Lord's grip on Gide's soul was first loosened. It was here that he first wriggled free.

It only took a few minutes—and it was no more than a taste of what it might mean to stop leading a double life—but one afternoon in a hollow in a sand dune outside the city walls one André, as it were, the twenty-three year old French virgin, finally turned and held out his hand to the André who had been stalking him for years.

Not that I'd have known from reading *If It Die* at the age of fourteen. My orange and white Penguin translation omitted virtually the entire incident, or at least what was significant about it. *Something* must have happened in the sand hills outside the town with the rascally, brown-skinned Ali, who flung himself down on his back with his arms stretched wide and looked across at André, laughing; *some thing* left traces of 'rapture' on André's face, he later said—he even suspected that his friend Paul noticed the change in his expression when they met up again afterwards; but what? In my edition of the book Ali's laughter faded away when it met no response, he said 'Goodbye, then', the word 'Omission' appeared coyly in italics and square brackets and then I read: 'In the meantime it was getting late. I had to join Paul.'

Nowadays I don't suppose any fourteen-year-old would have the slightest difficulty in picturing what must have happened between 'Goodbye, then' and 'In the meantime ...', but in the 1950s our teenaged imaginations were much less graphically informed. Yet even then I knew that whatever had been omitted was the key to something it was vital for me to understand. It had to do with leaving adolescence behind, with uncloaking the secret self that had been growing clammily inside you, although at fourteen, when I first read this passage, I was only just beginning to grow one (to be candid, more than one). And, whatever it was, it clearly had a lot to do with hoarsely whispering '*oui*' to Oscar Wilde a year later in Algiers.

It can hardly have been a matter of the translator's own prudishness because his loving translator was none other than Lytton Strachey's sister, Dorothy Bussy. The Stracheys and their circle, whatever their blind spots, were not prudish.

Dorothy Bussy met André Gide in the summer of 1918 while he was on his scandalous three-month visit to England with Marc Allégret. She was fifty-three, plain and married to a French artist the same age as Gide (forty-eight). Foolishly, Dorothy let herself fall passionately in love with André. (I say 'foolishly' and 'let herself', but obviously at the moment we're first smitten it doesn't feel like that, it feels like a gift from the gods, like being struck by lightning, a sudden, delicious illness, fate ... but then we begin to wilfully choreograph happenstance, turning it into something 'meant to be', so bear some responsibility.) Every morning he would cycle over to Cambridge from Grantchester where he and Marc had rooms and Dorothy would give him English lessons. He'd been reading English novelists and poets for most of his life, but his spoken English was bookish and needed brightening up. Remembering those first mornings in Cambridge, she wrote to him a year later, trying, as many of us do in this situation, to make sense of the feelings that had welled up in her, but not in him: 'I was just your dictionary and your grammar, convenient and helpful. And you had the same kind of friendly feeling for me that one has for a dictionary. I understood *that* perfectly.' We *understand*—of course we do: we are foolish, but not idiots—we know full well that our erotic feelings are finding no echo, but could we not somehow (by tomorrow, by next week) become a *loved* 'dictionary', then a *desired* 'dictionary'? We have so much to give, our intimacies could so easily thicken and spiral into something boundless. But 'you didn't notice', she goes on, 'that your dictionary had eyes and a heart, was watching you and wondering at you, was charmed and thrilled and shaken by you. I couldn't help it. Gide, I couldn't help it really. Aren't you the strangest and loveliest and the most disturbing thing I have ever come across in my life?'

And she loved him like that until the end. It's heartbreaking. Most moving of all was her reaction to the news about Elisabeth Van Rysselberghe's pregnancy, six years after she and Gide first met: 'It was excruciating,' Gide told Elisabeth's mother, 'it wasn't what I'd expected! I realised how terrible her passion was and that, when all was said and done, she hadn't given up in any way. Nevertheless, I was able to help her to regain her composure... I really do have the greatest admiration for her.' Yes, imprudent she may well have been, but there's no evidence that Dorothy Bussy was prudish. Was it the publishers who made the decision to mutilate the English text ('with the consent of the author', apparently)? The English are often scandalised by what they call 'indecency'—that's in fact what they nailed Oscar Wilde for, not homosexuality.

What actually happened between 'Goodbye, then' and 'In the meantime', as Dorothy knew from the full French text, was this:

> ... grasping the hand that he held out to me, I tumbled him to the ground. His laughter reappeared at once. He soon lost patience with the complicated knots of the cords that served as a belt; taking a small dagger out of his pocket, he sliced through the tangle at a stroke. The garment fell to the ground; he threw off his jacket and stood up straight, naked as a god. For a brief moment he held up his skinny arms to the sky, then, laughing, dropped down beside me. His body may have been burning hot, but to my hands it seemed as refreshingly cool as the shade. How beautiful the sand was! In the captivating splendour of the evening, what rays of sunlight clothed my joy!

It was not the euphoria he was to float away on in Algiers just over a year later, nor the ecstasy, the 'bitter-edged fever', he was finally to recapture with his cooing woodpigeon Ferdinand in 1907. It was just flesh. But it was a beginning. At this moment, in the sand dunes outside Sousse, one of Gide's selves began slowly to die and another one to spring to life. What is refreshing about

Gide's account of this incident, I think, is its lightness—there's no other word for it. At the end of the nineteenth century the archetypal seduction scene took place at night in a heavily-curtained, scented room. The faces glimpsed through the smoke from the tapers were pale and decadent, the gestures languid. Certainly nobody laughed. In Sousse it took place under a burning sun, without shame, although discreetly, in a hidden hollow in the sandhills. It was virile, not effete, frank, not veiled, open not furtive. And nobody felt miserable. This is what is shocking.

At the same time, it is not quite as virile or shocking as it might have been. 'Naked as a god . . . skinny arms . . . his body . . . burning hot'—this is not Walt Whitman. There is no 'love-flesh swelling and deliciously aching;/ Limitless limpid jets of love hot and enormous, quivering jelly of love, white-blow and delirious juice', as there was in Whitman's 'Sing the Body Electric' sixty-five years earlier. 'Naked as a god' sounds oddly feeble compared with Whitman's joy in 'feeling with the hand the naked meat of the body'. In other words, after reading the unedited account of Gide's awakening, which was first published in an edition of just twelve copies in 1920, we can picture little more of what happened than we could on reading Dorothy Bussy's, although this time we're left in no doubt that erotic intimacy did take place. It's almost irritatingly chaste, although not effete.

If It Die is a work of art. Facts were not Gide's only consideration as he wrote it. In 1910 (ten years before *If It Die* was published) he wrote some 'notes' on what happened in Sousse and here he was franker. He makes it plain that the boy propositioned him 'sweetly, caressingly', that as they sat looking at each other he, André, was almost burning with curiosity about what was going to happen, but he waited. They both waited, Ali sprawled on the sand, monkeying about, but alert to the possibilities. Finally, when André failed to make a move, Ali said: '*Adieu*, I go back, you not need me now', holding out his hand in farewell. This is where the published account kicks in: André throws him down, the boy takes a knife and cuts the cords on his trousers so that they fall to the ground and André murmurs in his ear: 'Do you want me to fu-- you?' ('*Tu veux que je t'enc.*') Ali says: 'If you like' and takes up the sort of position on the sand which makes it clear that he means what he said. 'I actually took no advantage of this,' Gide tells us. 'There was nothing violent about my desire; this child was delightful, amiable; there was nothing vicious or corrupt in his appearance or attitude.' And so presumably they simply lost themselves in pleasuring each other with their hands. That's what happened.

Whatever boyish sensual fulfilment was achieved, Gide was now forced to swivel and look his newly awakened secret self in the eye. In my terms, it was more a matter of inserting a key in the lock than of flinging the lid of a long-locked chest wide open. For that to happen, he needed the encouragement of somebody who had flung his own wide open years before: Oscar Wilde.

At twenty-three André was not thinking about doubles or sealed chests of hidden selves, any more than I was in Morocco. We were both thinking more romantically—and religiously—of bursting out of our tightly laced selves, of 'living fully' (as Gide begged God to let him do). It's never as easy as that, however. We're not butterflies encased in a chrysalis that we can simply burst out of in our lust to live. Gide always had a penchant for entomology.

In the meantime, having at last pressed his lips to a bit of flesh (which bits is left to our imagination—a neck or arm, probably), André made his way with Paul to Biskra in Algeria to see out the winter. At the end of the nineteenth century, Biskra, an oasis on the edge of the Sahara south-east of Algiers, was a place no traveller in North Africa with any flair would dream of neglecting to visit. Apart from anything else, in Biskra a man could harmlessly avail himself of the services of young girls from the Oulad Naïl tribe, renowned not only for their amber-skinned beauty, but for their curious custom of selling their bodies for a year or two to make money for their dowry. For two Parisian virgins in their early twenties, this was the perfect arrangement. After Sousse Gide was ready at last to explore his natural curiosity about making love to whoever might come to his bed. More than that: after what had happened in Sousse he could contemplate with more confidence marrying his adored, pious cousin, Madeleine. This is what most people find it so hard to understand: *now he could marry and stay married until death parted him from his wife.* It makes perfect sense to me: for the first time he could do what every man must eventually do *with honesty*. The marriage might be a mistake, as we've seen, but it would be an honest one.

It's true that he had some misgivings. Before becoming engaged, he decided to consult a doctor just to reassure himself that his 'desires' and marriage were perfectly compatible. The doctor, after listening to the young man's confession, offered him this startling piece of advice: 'You're saying that, while you love a young woman, you're hesitating to marry her, being aware at the same time of your tastes . . . Get married. Marry without fear. And you'll quickly realise that everything else exists only in your imagination. You give me the impression of a starving man who has been seeking to quench his hunger on pickled gherkins. Once you're married, you'll soon understand what the natural instinct is and come back to it spontaneously.'

Biskra was an important staging post on this path from pickled gherkins to marriage. Biskra was an education.

8.

BISKRA

Shortly before dawn one February morning in 1894—the sky had barely begun to redden—something memorable happened at the Hôtel de l'Oasis in Biskra. Having just arrived the night before from France in a panic over her son's health, Mme Gide, André's formidable mother, threw open her shutters to be greeted by a sight that wounded her to the core. Flitting across the terrace below was a dusky young woman, bracelets glinting on wrists and ankles. Stopping at the window of André's room, she whispered a few words to him when he appeared palely between the shutters and then vanished (in his words) like a ghost dispelled by a cock's crow. Mme Gide knew a woman of the night when she saw one.

André's mother was not just alarmed but shattered

by what she'd seen, although she managed to have her breakfast before summoning her son to her room to confirm her worst fears and vent her abundant grief. Her tears seem to have cauterised the wound of his sin very effectively—perhaps more effectively than she might have wished. Not only did he never sleep with Mériem ben Atala again, but, apart from a bit of inconclusive fumbling with Mériem's sister, it's not clear that he ever sinned with *any* woman again, not even his wife. Unless you count his brief coupling with Elisabeth van Rysselberghe on the beach at Hyères in 1922. Although this was certainly an unchurched coupling, it was hardly a matter of sinning: it was a friendly, and as it happened, effective act of insemination.

Sitting in the hushed public gardens across from the hotel over a century later—the very gardens André used to take slow morning walks in on that first visit, amongst the cassias, figs and palms, being still too ill to venture much farther afield—I found it hard to think myself back into that scene with any clarity. There was something impossibly melodramatic about it, almost unbelievable. All the same, it's a scene that stays vividly in the mind.

Admittedly, imagining yourself back in the town Gide knew and wrote about so often with such intense feeling, let alone trying to conjure up this unlikely scene, is not an easy task in general. Apart from anything else, Biskra, once Queen of the Desert, these days looks so dowdy. Yacoub had warned me back in Algiers that it was a small, shabby town of no conceivable interest to anybody, including himself, but this only whetted my appetite. Once there, I could see why he thought I was mad to go there.

If my 1895 *Handbook for Travellers in Algeria and Tunis* is to be believed, her charms were never exactly obvious. The author does concede that, despite a lack of 'beautiful scenery' or the 'splendid vegetation' which made Algiers so appealing, there could be no doubt that the dry climate was beneficial for some invalids, but that's the extent of his enthusiasm. (And, still spitting blood when he first arrived, Gide was certainly an invalid.) Another English traveller of the period, Alfred Pease, put it like this: 'Biskra must be wooed before she becomes really lovable.' But who would take the time? Writing less diplomatically just a few years later, the cross-dressing Swiss oblivion-seeker Isabelle Eberhardt remarked that the Queen of the Desert had been deposed and sullied and that her 'jewels are paste'. From her point of view, the whole of North Africa had been not just sullied but poisoned by the arrival of Europeans with their culture of spiritual emptiness. She may have had a point, but it's worth remembering that by this time she'd converted to Islam.

Eberhardt's views were colourful—they certainly produced some very purple prose—but hardly typical. At the time Gide first went to Biskra, it was a fashionable winter station of the highest order. ('Summer all winter' was one of its misleading slogans.) The Royal-Hôtel, for instance, owned by the Countess Le Marrois, where Gide stayed on his second visit, advertised itself as 'the meeting-place of distinguished tourists as well as of the French and foreign aristocracy'. They'd begun coming in droves after the Emperor Napoleon III gave the town his imprimatur in 1865 and just kept coming—counts and countesses, Oscar Wilde and Anatole France, artists such as Fromentin and Guillaumet, train-loads of what we'd nowadays call celebrities—until well into the 1930s. Now Biskra was left with the likes of me. Certainly at the Hôtel des Zibans, the only premier establishment in town these days according to Yacoub, I always dined alone. Perhaps I'd arrived too early in the season. Perhaps there is no season. My sparky guidebook to Algeria can't think of anything much to say about Biskra at all, except that the Carthaginians and Romans were once there and the gardens can offer 'a certain degree of coolness' in summer.

To judge by old postcards of Biskra, although the dromedaries, donkey traps and markets had disappeared from the streets, nothing much had changed in the public gardens by the time I arrived: the pathways cutting through the trees were still dusty and deserted, exactly as Gide had described them, apart from a few burnous-clad strollers and a man on a bicycle. Even the bell tower of the old French church still towered above the greenery, I noticed, although it was now some kind of Islamic library. It was easy to imagine the pale, thin Frenchman resting on one of the benches in the wintry sunshine pretending to read a book (Virgil, probably, or Homer) while waiting for a cooing woodpigeon to alight trustingly beside him, some bare-footed Bachir or Sadek or Mohammed with 'charmingly turned ankles and wrists'. In reality, the flitting Mériem, a prostitute from the Oulad Naïl tribe, was no more than a rite of passage for him, a carnal indulgence shared with his travelling companion Paul Laurens. (Erotic complicity can be so affirming in male friendship.) The two young men were simply losing their virginity in the time-honoured way while she was earning her dowry in the same spirit. Mutual exploitation of a very North African kind. Gide came to Mériem, he wrote, like a worshipper without an offering, and she was only 'bearable' because of her 'wildness'. Even as he made love to her on the Cardinal's bed at the Hôtel de l'Oasis (a relic from its days as a monastery), he imagined he was embracing the 'svelte, dark-skinned demon' he'd watched playing his drum in the café where he and Paul had first seen Mériem dance, her upper body rigid, her bracelets rattling on her swaying, snakelike arms, her bare feet beating out the rhythm of the half-naked demon's drums. He'd been partial to imps since his school days: he'd fallen in love with a boy dressed as an imp in black tights and spangles at a school ball. He'd gone dressed as a pastry cook. This sort of thing stays with you.

It had been in the street of the Oulad Naïl that he and Paul had watched Mériem dance. Swarming with local men as well as tourists, especially in the evening, this picturesque street with its unusual overhanging wooden balconies and abundance of smoky Moorish tea-houses was not, as my old guidebook puts it, 'a sight to be recommended to English ladies'. However, the girls in their gaily embroidered tunics, silk sashes and heavy jewellery—bracelets, anklets, diadems, necklaces—sitting in doorways waiting for customers were as important an attraction for many Europeans as the dry climate. They featured on postcards as prominently as the town's souks, thermal baths and luxury hotels.

In a word, André Gide in the gardens was something I could vividly picture, even a century later. While the tearful scene at the hotel smacked of a costume drama, André loitering in the public gardens across from the hotel was perfectly imaginable. Well, here I was loitering in them myself. I'd have liked to wander in them in the moonlight as well, to be honest, whether to drink it or not, I'd have liked to see the silvered leaves of the olive trees that he took such pleasure in on certain nights, to listen for a flute in the darkness as he did, keeping an eye out for boys as dark as violets, but I didn't dare. Just venturing as far south as Biskra across the Aurès mountains seemed foolhardy enough. Certainly the alarmingly moustachioed airport police found my presence there all too curious, taking me aside for some lengthy questioning before letting me leave the terminal to find a taxi.

It wasn't particularly difficult, either, to imagine Gide on his long walks into the nearby villages of N'Msid and Bab-el-Derb on the edge of the palm groves. On every visit to Biskra he would make a point of escaping as often as he could from the French quarter, taking the road south to these villages on the very rim of the desert. Nowadays their tangled, mud-walled lanes are simply the untidy fringe of the city itself. A century ago, however, these brown and yellow, vaguely sullen villages on the edge of the oasis—the only splash of colour is the pale aquamarine of the mosques—were a temptation to young André, an enchanted labyrinth of secret high-walled gardens and hidden courtyards, crumbling away here and there, as they still do, to let the lush, sweet-smelling green of the palm groves invite him to wander off into their cooler depths. It was here that he would prowl alone, leaving Paul to his own devices, seeking out the company of goatherds amongst the date palms, listening to the thin, monotonous rustling of their flutes, an echo of the wind soughing over the sands further south. There were no piping goatherds amongst the date palms the day I went strolling in N'Msid and Bab-el-Derb, just blue plastic bags snared on every bush—on almost every blade of grass, it seemed to me—but all the same a hint remained of what must have enticed André to lose himself in this maze of silent, dusty streets interlaced with fingers of brilliant green, stretching, if you cared to follow them, all the way to the first stones of the Sahara.

Having walked there myself, I now have some inkling of what he meant when he said that once you start walking on the edge of the desert, you can't stop. No matter how tired you are (you can be practically toppling over with fatigue), no matter how anxious you feel about getting lost, you can't stop or turn around. You sink into a trance, you become drunk on space. Whether following a track through the endless date palms, or heading out onto the scrubby plain beyond, you find yourself walking on and on, step after step after step, with no thought of where you're going, no thought of anything. Thought peels off—you see, you smell, you hear, but thought starts flaking off as soon as you step from the road into the greenery, while time begins to bend, curving round as you leave the clatter of the street behind until, silently, you feel it snap. It could go on like this all the way to Touggourt, to Tamanrasset, even Togo, you could drift like this all the way to the Congo. In some ways it's a wonder André ever made it back to the Hôtel de l'Oasis before midnight.

That first winter in Biskra with his friend Paul, though, fresh from Sousse, the hours of darkness had their own attraction back in town, however strong the temptation was to saunter around the native quarters 'savouring the moonlight like a sorbet'. On the way back he liked to rest in a small, mud-brick hut on the edge of the oasis at Bab-el-Derb, an end-of-the-day sort of place, he said, where ginger tea was served in the gathering silence as the panting day breathed its last. All he could hear as he gazed out at the desert at dusk was the sound of a flute's ecstasy. Ah! Those four-holed shepherds' flutes! Ennui and longing. The old Attic fantasy again. This was easy to picture as well, despite the fact that the café itself must be long gone and all I could hear as dusk gathered was the whine of motorbikes and the dogs guarding the orchards amongst the palm groves starting to yap.

He didn't dally in Bab-el-Derb, though, because back in town on that first visit there was a café which drew him into its cramped gloom night after night. In point of fact, it was more what the French used to call an *échoppe*—a dimly lit room giving onto the street, where henna was sold by day while, once darkness fell, young men would meet to play a game of cards (monte, as a rule) or sometimes draughts and smoke a hooka. André spent almost every evening there that first winter, while Paul amused himself in the newly opened casino. Years later Gide wondered why he went there with such devotion: after all, he didn't smoke hashish, didn't play cards or draughts and 'wasn't exactly in love' with any of the boys. No, not with Bachir, Mohammed or any of their friends, but he *was* in love with the feel and mood of the place, with its shadowy quiet—with its chanciness, I suppose, as well as with the boys' slim, graceful youthfulness. What he meant, I think, was that he wasn't troubled by a desire for this one or that, but floated pleasurably on a cloud of sensual awareness in their company. And why not? It's what I sometimes feel myself in the souks of Tunis or Fez—a *volupté*, as the French might call it, a delight in the effortless physical beauty of so many of the figures crossing my path, without any need to translate my delight into enjoyment. Sometimes. Perhaps as you grow older that's what happens. It might be how you feel when you're very young as well and can't quite picture what enjoyment might entail. André was twenty-four by this time, but he was still, as we know, almost entirely without experience—apart from his brief adventure in the sand hills outside Sousse. Enjoyment was still a hazy concept.

The scene in this café was one I could also imagine without too much trouble, even if there were few signs of this kind of gathering place, as far as I could see, in modern Biskra. There's a wary, standoffish feel to Algerian towns today, even in the cafés, quite unlike the easy, almost playful friendliness—or relaxed insolence—you find in Tunisia. But elsewhere I have often sat in cafés amongst men smoking hookas, admiring their slender charm, exchanging smiles, making small talk with whoever sat next to me, losing all sense of who I was or where I'd come from and letting minutes balloon into hours, without trying to harpoon anyone.

What it was almost impossible for me to transport myself back into, however, was the tearful scene of outrage and grief in Mme Gide's hotel room. It made some kind of sense, I'm not denying that—the Calvinist mother aghast at her son's flagrant sinfulness—but it was too stagy, almost operatic, for me to feel any serious connection with it. It reminded me of the story of Gide's grandmother fainting in horror when she discovered an altar to the Virgin Mary in a cupboard in her son's bedroom: a world where this could happen is simply hard to take seriously now.

An altar to the Virgin Mary would be the least of a French grandmother's worries these days, however staunchly Protestant she was. Compared to some of the things she'd probably find while rummaging through his cupboard, she might even find an altar (any altar) strangely reassuring.

Yet it is memorable, this scene at the Hôtel de l'Oasis, but not because it's a story about being caught out breaking the rules. Who hasn't been caught out breaking the rules? What happened that February morning in Biskra is unforgettable because it's the quintessential 'cusp' experience: in Mme Gide's room the arc of André's pious childhood swooped in from across the sea to meet the arc of his newly unlocked self, still raw at that juncture, still revelling in its nakedness. It both laid bare (to him, although not to his mother) the double life he'd been leading, freeing him to say *'oui'* to Oscar Wilde in Algiers the following winter, and warned him that soon he would have to reclothe himself and eventually marry. Not just anyone, a homosexual is never likely to marry just anyone, but specifically his cousin, Madeleine Rondeaux. Now, after his experience in Sousse and this encounter with his outraged mother, he knew that his instinct had not betrayed him: the only woman who could be his wife was his angelic cousin, Madeleine Rondeaux.

No wonder Gide kept coming back to Biskra almost obsessively for years. He came back to Biskra, this town whose charms were so limited, even in its heyday, the following year straight after his adventure in the casbah in Algiers, he came back on his honeymoon with Madeleine the year after that, and again in 1899 and in 1900. He even bought a property in Biskra not far from the magnificent walled garden of Count Landon de Longueville. His last visit was in 1945. He didn't come for the invigorating dry climate, the thermal baths or the fashionable hotels. He came above all, it seems to me, especially on his honeymoon, because that's where the double that had been prowling in the shadows for so long first found itself blinking shyly in the light. He came back to remember oblivion.

On reflection, I'm sure that's why I, too, constantly go back to North Africa, reliving its colours, smells and sounds, replaying in my mind the encounters of decades ago: to remember just *being*, 'unsullied', in Isabelle Eberhardt's terms, by everything that has formed me. It's hard for me to think of where else that is possible. On my first visit to Morocco, as for Gide in Biskra, nothing particularly dramatic happened for me to remember—my casbah experience, like his, occurred on my second visit the following year. And, if I'm honest with myself, I don't even much like North Africa, I always leave disillusioned: one oasis begins to look like another after a while, one stretch of sand dunes is indistinguishable from the last, the cities, even Tunis, are for the most part chaotic, grubby and dangerous, the religion is too all-pervasive for my taste, the unrelieved maleness of every encounter tiring, the disdain for almost every value I hold dear numbing after a while... yet I go back. To disentangle myself from the educated clutter of my everyday life. To be naked again. To relive that moment when for the first time what had been kept invisible began to show through. For many Europeans with a veiled second self North Africa is still the perfect vantage point to let this happen. For some it might be an ashram in India or some remote village in Borneo, even a Greek island might fit the bill for others, but for me it is North Africa.

Unmediated being (to give it a pompous title) is always slithering out of our grasp at home. We look for it in food, drink, sex and lying in the sun (all the things the tourist brochures promise us wherever we're thinking of going) and I can't help thinking that unmediated being is what people are probably also looking for at rock concerts and in gospel choirs, at the gambling tables, at football finals, riding surfboards, even on roller-coasters and on bushwalks. But it's momentary—it has to be momentary, you can't live like that, nobody would want to. It's like the show stopper at the end of an exciting night at the theatre: you want it to go on forever, and you'll also shatter into a thousand pieces if it doesn't stop *now*. It's not the sex in itself that we crave, or the smoked salmon and strawberries and cream, it's not lying on a beach in the sun or screaming ourselves hoarse at men chasing a ball, but the whoosh of emptiness—'crazy wisdom', as Daniel calls it. A splash of divine madness.

North Africa is where, almost magically, this still seems possible—for a few days, a week, a month. I understand exactly the quality of Gide's joy on his second visit to Biskra when he found that his ground-floor window in the Royal-Hôtel gave directly onto the street instead of a terrace watched over by his mother. 'In one bound,' he wrote in his diary,

> I could jump through it. Sadek . . . and a few of the others from the old town used to come and relax with me during Ramadan before going back to their village. I would have dates, cakes, syrups and jams for them. It would be night-time. Sadek would play his flute and we found it easy to stay silent for a long time. At night I closed only the shutters. All the outside noises came into the room. Every morning they woke me before dawn and I would

walk to the edge of the desert to watch the sunrise . . .

This is a scene rich in erotic possibility, food, music (and silence)—even the sun makes an appearance here—but its power lies in that original image: the window he could jump through in one bound. At home it's never like that. Nor should it be.

As in this scene, I suspect that when we want to burn off all those clusters of self-awareness, want to taste life in all its rawness once more, there's an infantile impulse at work. Like Gide at the Royal-Hôtel, we're playing at being children again. We want to be given the chance to start afresh. We're almost certainly deluding ourselves: new beginnings are almost always an illusion. All the same, it's a temptation to believe they're possible, especially at those moments when we realise we're not now ever going to have the life we wanted. Perhaps if we go back to the beginning again . . . ? But no, in reality it never works. From the moment we get out of the taxi at Tunis or Casablanca airport to fly home, the weight of all those years—that mass of things ordering our everyday selves: our habits of mind and speech, the plethora of small proprieties, the memory of what we know and believe, our whole history since our school days—sinks down on us again, muffling something joyous and innocent in us, telling us where to go, what to say, how to behave, who we properly are. After days or weeks of spiritual spaciousness, as the doors to the departures concourse snap shut behind us, we feel gripped again by our old 'moral agoraphobia' (to quote the Oscar Wilde character in *The Immoralist*).

All at once there's language everywhere, too—the signs, the booming announcements and commands, the displays of books and newspapers, the crowds chattering in English, French, German. It's a shock after the restless silence we've been inhabiting (unavoidably, unless we speak Arabic). On the wall of my cubicle in the airport washroom there is startlingly blunt information about someone called Guy Dupont and his predilection for camels. 'Air France announces the departure of flight 1285 to Paris. Passengers should go directly to gate 51.' Meekly I go. 'Air France paging Mr Michel Lambert, passenger to Paris. Your aircraft is ready for immediate departure. If you do not go to gate 51 now, your luggage will be unloaded.' Has Michel Lambert fled in panic back to the perfumed chaos of the medina? Is he already on a minibus heading back to the desert where camels are just camels? He's probably lost in the maze of duty-free shops, but I can fantasise.

As we nose up into the blue-brown haze, I always stare in rueful silence at the back of the seat in front of me: I've actually forgotten nothing. And to be brutally honest with myself, although I came to North Africa to forget, there was one thing I was particularly careful not to misplace: my ticket home.

Some of us clearly have more to forget than others. Young André, for example, even in his early twenties, already had an abundance of cultural baggage to leave behind, he was staggering under the weight of it by the time he reached Biskra. He knew the Latin and Greek poets off by heart; his diary is peppered with references to writers and thinkers such as Leibniz, Fichte, Goethe, Dickens and Turgenev, as well as the whole canon of French thought and letters from Rabelais to the Symbolist poets whose soirées he frequented. And, better than any of these writers (he said), he knew Chopin, the composer most likely to induce impure thoughts in the young, according to his mother; and he knew his Bible back to front, naturally. He was the educated Western man incarnate. Yet no sooner did he glimpse the coast of Africa than he was telling anyone who would listen that he wanted to throw all this baggage aside. 'Culture,' as he wrote in *The Immoralist*, 'born of life, killing life.'

It was easy for him to say. It's easy to turn up your nose at the accumulated achievements of Western culture—to drive straight past Agrigentum, for instance, as the Immoralist does, without bothering to visit the most spectacular Doric temples in Sicily, to spare Paestum, one of the best preserved monuments of Magna Grecia (three stars in my Michelin guide) no more than a passing glance on the way to Naples, as he does—when you have an intimate knowledge of their history and can afford to come back any time you like. In Syracuse, Athens' rival at the height of its power and an archeological wonderland, the Immoralist spends all his days (and no doubt most of his nights) down in the old port, consorting in its muddy alleys and stinking taverns with dockers, vagabonds and drunken sailors—'the lowest dregs of society'. 'What need did I have to understand their language when I could taste it in the flesh of my whole body?' he asks in a way I find a touch overripe. 'I'd have liked to roll under the table with them to wake up only at the first sad shiver of dawn.' (This proved impractical because his ailing wife was waiting for him back at their hotel.)

To get away with this sort of thing you have to be either oblivious of the treasures on the hill above or wealthy enough not to care how you spend your time and money. How easy it must have been to dismiss, as Gide did on his trip up the Nile, the crowds of ordinary tourists 'swooning' like 'imbeciles' over the giant granite boulders of Aswan that they'd read about in their guidebooks. (What sparked his contempt, it's worth noting, was the fact that these boulders were 'famous', and in landscapes nothing irritated him more than layers of interpretation. Art was another matter. In fact, while he was in Aswan he was reading the *Aeneid* in the original Latin. In art, interpretation had an honoured place.) My point is simply that you can't cast 'culture, decency and morality' aside unless you're cloaked in it in the first place.

Menalcas, the Oscar Wilde character in *The Immoralist*, sums it up pithily. 'You seem to lack the sense of something, dear Michel,' he says to his young friend.

'A sense of morality, perhaps...'

'Oh, simply the sense of ownership... And for a person who has no sense of ownership, you seem to own a great deal.'

Exactly. All the same—and this is such a Protestant touch in Gide's young Immoralist—his essential point is curiously valid: his education (and inherited wealth) are simply *there*, part of what he has been given, not something he has greedily striven for, so they can be enjoyed without guilt or hypocrisy in France, where their roots are ancient; once he is on foreign soil, however, he might quite legitimately seek to peel them off and rejoice in his new-found nakedness.

Which is what he did—what many of us have been tempted to do—as soon as he reached Tunis. Obviously the stranglehold of 'culture, decency and morality' on the local inhabitants was, and is, as strong as anything Gide was escaping from back in France; but from his point of view, fresh off the boat from Marseilles (and even from mine, when I went there nearly a century later), it seemed that life could be lived there with a kind of immediacy impossible at home. That, I think, is the key to our fascination: the lure of unmediated experience.

This is how he remembered Tunis in *The Immoralist*:

> Tunis! The light is more abundant than strong. The shadows are still full of it. The air itself seems like a luminous liquid bathing everything, you dive into it, you swim in it. This land of sensual pleasures satisfies your desire but does not appease it. Each time your desire is satisfied, it is sharpened. [This reminds me of Oscar Wilde on the subject of cigarettes.]
>
> A land taking a holiday from works of art. I despise those who are unable to recognise beauty until it has been transcribed and interpreted. The Arabs have the admirable quality of living their art, singing it and letting it seep into their lives bit by bit from day to day; they don't pin it down, don't embalm it in any work of art. This is the cause and effect of the absence of great artists . . . I have always believed that great artists were those who dared to give the right to beauty to things so natural that they make those who see them say: 'How could I not have realised before that this too is beautiful?'

This is obviously a very condescending, European take on Tunis, but, to be fair, it wasn't only Arabs he condescended to. And, to give him his due, even today the European visitor to Tunis will notice the absence of bookshops, art galleries, theatres or concert halls of the kind you'd find in abundance in any city of the same size in Europe. The posters outside the cinemas advertise nothing apart from lust and carnage, the crowds in the trams, the parks and cafés simply *look*, nobody seems to be reading. In the waiting room at Biskra airport, for instance, nobody at all was reading anything, not even a newspaper. Everyone was just looking around edgily. (The threat of something unpleasant happening hangs in the air at every airport, I admit, especially in Algeria.) Perhaps 'culture, decency and morality' are invisible to us because in North Africa, as in medieval Europe, they are the province of religious institutions. We think as we jostle with the crowds in the medina or wander off into some palm grove on the edge of the Sahara that we're experiencing life in its unwrapped form. At first it's unbearably exciting. Forget the Ninth Symphony—there's a shepherd playing a flute in the darkness. Who needs Matisse? In front of you is a turquoise door edged in black. Beside these simple white burnouses, the extravagant creations of Milanese designers seem bogus, almost trashy. Here, you think to yourself, there are no tangled doubts, just faith, no history, just stories—what history could a Touareg on a camel have? (Well, we all go to Carthage, naturally we do, usually on our second day in Tunis, but that's different, that's *real* history, those ruins are ours.) It's rarely like that in Stockholm or San Francisco. It's not even often like that in Istanbul or Cairo (which is probably why these two cities failed to seduce André Gide). And it's never like that in Switzerland.

It's all very well to cast off your European trappings and stand naked in the Tunisian sun, but what do you *do* with your newly naked self? I'm not talking about whether or not you go to the Bardo Museum to admire the Roman mosaics, or have coffee and a sandwich at the Café de Paris, watching the smart set at play, or even somewhere more colourful in the medina. I'm talking about how to spend time in a way that means anything. At the end of *The Immoralist*, Michel, marooned in an Algerian village, his wife safely buried nearby at El Kantara, complains of suffering from his pointless liberty. He can't seem to start living a real life. Enjoyment follows too closely upon desire here, he says, his yielding to happiness is too unvarying, his days of leisure are becoming intolerable, his mind is dulled by the endless empty blueness . . . *he would like to begin all over again*. Choking the life out of your habitual self is one thing—breathing life into your primitive, unschooled self quite another.

Travel to places like Algeria or Tunisia is like temporary suicide: it has all the advantages of killing yourself with none of the disadvantages. For the first few days I admit I'm tempted to escape from time to time into a comforting book—a detective novel set in a Yorkshire vicarage, for instance, is always reassuring—grasping onto it like a passenger on a departing ocean liner clutching a streamer. It stretches and eventually snaps and I drift off into the blue. Water, sky, earth, palm trees. The husky music of Arabic. Needy eyes. Then the gnawing begins. It's all too *thin*. In the public gardens in Biskra on my last afternoon I tried to let my untutored self take over one last time—to banish the mind, bend time, forget my lines, as it were, and become a small, hungry animal again, all eyes and ears and nose, ready for anything. For an hour or two it worked, but I can only forget so much: I *have* read Tolstoy, Flaubert, Virgil and the Bible, I *have* been to the Greek ruins in Syracuse, to Herculaneum and Pompeii, I know Matisse from Monet, and I have admired, for that matter, the boulders at Aswan. All these things are part of the mosaic of who I am. I can take a holiday from it, but I can't just throw all that off and stand around naked wondering what to do next. Living in the moment can be refreshing in short bursts, but it affords me no lasting pleasure: there's something too slippery about moments, they swirl around like water in the sink and then go whoosh down the plughole, leaving you stranded again. So in the end I felt slightly bored. The milky trickling of an oud is all very well, but once you've heard Beethoven it's never quite enough. To have desire followed so immediately by enjoyment is a delight, but I need to love. Love, as Mme Gide was there to remind her son, is a matter of cultivation. Love is what you do at home. All the same, even if bliss was fast turning to listlessness, I was glad that Yacoub hadn't followed me to Biskra, as he'd said he might, despite considering it the dullest town in Algeria. If Yacoub had turned up (he'd claimed to have a cousin he might be visiting that weekend in Constantine, just a few hours' drive to the north) we'd have filtered Biskra through skeins of talk. I'd have hardly seen *Biskra* at all. He'd have been wearing something snappy, no doubt, that he'd picked up on his last trip to Paris, he'd have told me what the Romans called the settlement two thousand years ago, and all about the Hillalians and Hafsids and Merinids from Fez. We'd have gone out to the oasis at Sidi Oqba, talking all the way, to see the ancient mosque there ('parts of it dating from the eighth century'—I could hear him saying it in his faultless French), and he'd have told me in fascinating detail all about Oqba Ibn Nafaâ, who is buried there and who had founded Kairouan, as a matter of fact, and gone on to take Islam to the farthest reaches of the world (Tangier at the time): only the ocean prevented him from forcing every nation beyond Africa 'who knew not God' to worship Him alone or die. If I'd asked, he'd probably have translated the Cufic script on one of the pillars of the mosque. And he'd have done it all with his usual faint astonishment that I could be so ignorant, mixed with just a hint of displeasure at any too obvious interest, as if he suspected that I was being condescending. In a word, I'd have thoroughly enjoyed his company, but he straddled our two worlds too comfortably, I'd have felt far too much at home. And it would have made it even harder to explain to him, as eventually I must, why I was there.

◆

Back at the airport the police officer who had let me out onto the street when I first arrived was lying in wait for me to reappear. Had I enjoyed myself in Biskra? Oh, yes, very much, I said. He stroked his moustache thoughtfully. I could see that even he found this curious. And who exactly was this André Gide I'd been trying to find? Well, not *find*, I said, he'd been dead for over fifty years, but . . . well, he was a writer who'd spent a lot of time in Biskra and I wanted to see for myself the town that had meant so much to him. He looked at me with his dark, bruised eyes and I could see that he thought I was slightly loopy.

'Have you ever been to Tonga?' he asked, after a short pause, idly flicking through the pages of my passport.

'No, I can't say I have. Why do you ask?'

'I've always wanted to go to Tonga. It's been my dream since I was a boy. Do you know if it's easy to get there from where you live?'

'Very easy, I should think. A few hours by plane.'

'Then why haven't you been there?' He flicked through my passport again. 'Canada, France, Russia, Japan—you must be very rich, yet you've never been to Tonga. Why not?' He waited patiently for me to explain myself. There was nothing I could say. I knew why, but no words came. He handed me back my passport. 'If you can, do go there,' he said. 'It's paradise.'

9.

SO BE IT

> ... I've made up my mind to write at random. It's not an easy undertaking because the pen (it's a fountainpen) lags behind my thoughts. Now, it's vital not to foresee what one is about to say, that's true. But there's always a bit of play-acting in it ... If I feel like contradicting myself, I shall without a qualm. I won't strive for 'coherence'. But I won't affect incoherence, either. Hidden away beyond logic there is a way of thinking that is more important to me at this point ... I aim to amuse myself here ... Perhaps at my age it's permissible to let oneself go a bit. *Amen*. (Which means, I believe: so be it!)
>
> *André Gide, on the first page of his last book,*
> So Be It *or* The Chips are Down

Naples, June 2007

He's suspended in mid-air, this naked youth. Arms outstretched, long, graceful legs pointing skywards, he's little more than an ochre streak about to slice like a scimitar into a bluish sea. Yet he's unforgettable. He's just a brushstroke on the lid of an ancient Greek tomb, the work of a few moments, probably, but of all the paintings you see at Paestum—the depictions of drinking parties, a boy playing an *aulos*, men singing and even indulging in a spot of erotic play—nothing stays in the mind like 'The Diver'.

He's been caught, this young man (or so they tell us), plummeting from life into the sea of death. For two and a half thousand years he's been plunging without moving an inch towards the afterlife—it's quite literally a suspended sentence. On second thoughts, he's not plunging so much as *hanging*. He's just leapt into the air, he's just this moment kicked his legs up behind him, he's not quite yet falling. He's mortal yet eternal, doomed yet unchanging, caught by the artist at an ecstatic pinnacle. Is that why he wrenches the heart?

Or is he nothing more than a boy diving into water? For all we really know, the dead man who was buried in this colourful tomb may have simply liked splashing about at the seaside, as he apparently liked noisily carousing with his friends, if the other scenes painted on his coffin are anything to go by. Called in to give him something to remember on his final journey, some local dauber may have simply thought to himself: 'I'm sick of half-naked men lying about on cushioned benches playing the lyre. I know, I'll do something with a beach motif.'

From up here on the rooftop terrace of the Hôtel Britannique I can't see as far as Paestum. It's half a day's journey away, beyond the hills above Sorrento to the south. I do have a sweeping view of the Bay of Naples, though, if I lean out far enough, as well as of Capri, gleaming in the sun out to sea. (The waiter who brought me my coffee claimed that it's Ischia, but I'm sure it's Capri. Not that it matters. The coffee is excellent, the waiter sleek.) The white ferries and pleasure boats heading out to the islands, or for the docks far below me near the Royal Palace, dot the bay like seagulls. From high up here Naples looks spectacularly beautiful. There's a brazen extravagance about it, sprawled like this around its sweeping bay, palazzo piled on palazzo, almost inviting violation. Almost anyone you can think of did violate it: the Greeks, the Romans, the barbarians, the Spaniards, the Bourbons. No wonder wealthy Romans came here on vacation to eat, drink and debauch themselves in the sun, it's the perfect setting. Yet I only have to cross the road in front of the hotel and start picking my way down the staircases into its clogged streets and laneways towards the sea to find myself engulfed by its chaos and filth. To tell the truth, I don't much like Naples. Its extravagance goes against the grain. I wonder if I should perhaps move further south—to somewhere on the Amalfi coast, for example, where everything is more safely picturesque. Still, I should give it a chance, I've only just arrived. Perhaps I'm just in the morose sort of mood Gide once described so accurately on arriving in Algiers from Marseilles: 'The moment when I most frantically desire to leave a city is when I've just arrived. What squalor! What wretchedness! What a let-down! What mediocre "promises of happiness"! Or more precisely: how few promises and what mediocre happiness!' It was six-thirty in the morning when he made that diary entry, and he was feeling old (he was not quite sixty), exhausted after the crossing from Marseilles and slightly worried about a pain in his left lung. The next day he realised that it wasn't just a matter of fatigue and the pain in his lung: 'Above all,' he wrote, 'my low spirits came from not having shaved, my dirty collar and unwashed clothes... A phone-call from Montherlant came just at the right moment like a cockcrow to put to flight these twilight ghosts. I went back up to my room to wash, shave, change my underwear, my clothes, my thoughts.' It's pathetic, really, when you're travelling, how sensitive you are to such petty things as these. Clean underwear and a splash of eau de cologne and almost anywhere can look enticing.

Naples unsettled Stendhal, it now occurred to me, yet you'd have thought his enthusiasm for travelling (in style, of course) was inexhaustible. He remarked in his *Promenades dans Rome* that by the time he got here, he wished he could have found the river Lethe and, drinking deeply, forgotten everything he'd seen in Italy and then started travelling all over again. In other words, by the time he got here he knew Naples and Italy too well to fall again under their spell. More than that: he knew life too well. 'Alas, in one respect,' he wrote, 'all knowledge is like old age, whose worst symptom is the *knowledge of life* that prevents one from becoming passionate about anything, from behaving madly over nothing ... Instead of admiring the ruins of the temple of Jupiter, as I did twenty-six years ago, my imagination is chained to all sorts of stupid things I've read about it.' In the same vein his contemporary, the writer, diplomat and statesman Chateaubriand, once complained that once you've seen Niagara, there are no more waterfalls. 'My memory never stops opposing one journey to another, one mountain range to another, one river to another, one forest to another, and my life is destroying my life.' Lamentably, although he died at eighty, he'd seen Niagara at the age of twenty-three.

Last night I made an attempt to behave madly over nothing by going down to the *lungomare*, the seafront down the hill from my hotel, where the waiter, Giovanni, hinted that on Sunday evenings I'd find a sort of carnival by the sea: food stalls and sideshow attractions swarming with hawkers, buskers and fashionable *flâneurs*. On a warm summer's evening, while watching the local youths diving off the breakwater, you might even find yourself jostled by half-naked skaters and joggers. Giovanni didn't phrase it quite like that, but he made it sound as if a stroll by the water might lift my spirits. Perhaps I'd be swept up by someone louche but snappily dressed, someone at a loose end, perched provocatively on the seawall on the lookout for a bit of tomfoolery to pass the time, and be driven off to 'hit the city's coolest restaurants, bars and clubs for some designer *dolce vita*' (in the words of my guidebook, which unfailingly looks on the bright side). But I'd seen it all before. At a certain point in life, like Stendhal and Chateaubriand, one has. Everything feels repackaged. The crêpe and ice-cream wagons, the miniature train, the hoopla stall, the Africans selling belts and fake Louis Vuitton handbags—even the gangs of teenagers in T-shirts emblazoned with jaunty slogans in English (i love beer, fuck work and so on)—I'd seen and heard and smelt it all before hundreds of times. It felt like the umpteenth performance of a circus act I'd first thrilled to when I was five. Would nothing transformingly beautiful ever happen again? Besides, everyone was sauntering about in tight packs of family and friends. There was plenty of heat, but no electricity. All I ended up feeling was old. I never feel old in Tunisia, which is where my river Lethe runs. Of course, I *am* old. Well, not *old*, but at the wrong end of middle-aged. Unlike 'The Diver' in Paestum I've passed my ecstatic pinnacle. I'm falling.

Interestingly enough, not far from here, on the way to Paestum at Salerno (across the bay and around the corner, at the far end of the Amalfi coast), there was once a famous medical school specialising in working out regimens for holding old age at bay. There being little left in Salerno these days worth more than a passing glance, the museum dedicated to the history of the Scuola Medica Salernitana is a fascinating place to pass the time while waiting for the bus to Paestum. Although ideas about ageing changed enormously over the thousand years of the School's existence, at its height in the eleventh and twelfth centuries the best advice it could come up with was to apply its rules of hygiene, using various potions recommended by the ancients, and to stay healthy for as long as possible. This was considered a duty to God at the time, the body being the earthly instrument of the soul.

All over Western Europe, wherever the School's influence was felt, men and women nonetheless continued to turn into puckered, rheumy old doddards, just as they'd always done, sinking at an alarmingly early age into smelly decrepitude before toppling gnarled and half-blind into their graves, often with a hefty push from the younger members of their families. Staying healthy may have staved off this painful decline for a few years, but it was no antidote to ageing.

Even today, with all our cunning devices for keeping the body limber longer, we rot. There is no antidote to ageing. We can stretch our skin, dye our hair, ease the pain in our joints and keep most of our teeth, but gradually we change for the worse. That's what ageing means, after all: changing for the worse. Bit by bit the butterfly turns into a worm. Burrowing back into the dark, it one day dissolves into the earth.

In the centre of Naples yesterday I saw almost no worms at all. On the via Chaia and the via Santa Lucia, for instance, where the young and expensively preserved gather, I saw mostly butterflies. On the via Toledo, the street that in 1817 Stendhal called 'the most crowded, the gayest street in the universe', there were a few worms decked out as butterflies, flitting in and out of the boutiques and patisseries, and the odd clutch of elderly foreigners off the cruise ships enjoying a few hours' sightseeing in designer leisure wear, but you really have to prowl around the gloomy back streets higher up the hillside to see the ancient unadorned. There, in the shadows, hunched crones bicker with each other from window to window and old men totter around the narrow streets beneath the lines of washing, grunting greetings to each other and toothlessly discussing football. Staying agile, smooth-skinned and upright is too costly an affair for the denizens of the *quartieri spagnoli*. Neither worm nor butterfly, I felt largely invisible all day, a kind of momentary blur on the crowded pavements.

Gide didn't hide away in the shadows or burrow into the earth as he grew old—and he grew *very* old indeed. He seems to have had a remarkably good old age, too. It's one of the things that make me warm to him. Naturally enough, at times he felt lonely, especially after the death of Madeleine, the 'other voice' in his dialogue with life. He had his daughter Catherine, conceived on the beach at Hyères-Plage, eventually even grandchildren, and friends who hungered for his company, but that's never quite the point. At some juncture it suddenly hits you that when you talk almost nobody knows what you're talking about any more. The crowd, *your* crowd, it now strikes you, is beginning to thin out. The new crowd, sometimes with bright smiles on their unlined faces, basically wants you to move aside, get out of the way, stand back against the wall with all the other stragglers and leave the floor to them. Gide, as one might expect, was not inclined to follow their instructions.

Naturally enough, the 'minor infirmities' of his advanced years made him feel wretched from time to time: he complained that his limbs went numb, for instance, that his skin itched, making it hard to sleep, and that he'd grown so scrawny towards the end that in the colder months he couldn't get warm. In the early spring of 1943, when he was seventy-three, he said that he had to put on and take off various undergarments and vests at least twenty times a day to avoid catching cold and, if he revolted against this 'servitude', he unfailingly caught cold and felt miserable for days. 'But I have to keep on living,' he wrote in his diary, 'while telling myself over and over again that it could be much worse.' (And in 1943 it undoubtedly could.)

It wasn't facile optimism, however, that gave him

what was on the whole a good old age. It wasn't some sort of Pollyanna-ish 'I must count my blessings', nor was it some shallow attempt to stay 'young at heart'.

(Here comes Giovanni with another jug of coffee and some almond biscuits. His long, black locks dangle across his face as he bends to rest his tray on the table beside my chair. For some reason I think of hyacinths. Hair like hyacinths. Odysseus had hair like hyacinths. So Greek. Apollo made hyacinths spring up on the spot where he'd carelessly sliced the head off his beloved, Hyacinthus, with a discus. For a moment Giovanni admires the view he's seen a thousand times, then with a nod strides off. The silver disk of his tray flashes in the sun. My mind drifts back to the ageing Gide.)

A *thick* life, that was Gide's secret. It's an odd word in English, but one he used over and over again. A good old age in his case, if his diaries are any guide, had something to do with an unfailing appetite for the tightly woven, for turning the basic melodies that shaped his mind from childhood into sonatas, concertos, symphonies, operas, ballets. This makes it sound as if he strove to turn the simple into the complex and grand, but that wasn't what he did at all: it was more a matter of playing with almost endless variations on fundamental themes by reading more widely, rereading with greater attention, staying curious, living fearlessly (unlike Madeleine) and acquiring new passions. This is not at all the same thing as 'making yet another pot of tea with the same leaves', which the art historian Bernard Berenson said was an overwhelming temptation in old age. That would have left life tasting 'thin'. From his teenaged years until his death André Gide ceaselessly enriched his spirit, striving to make the Narcissus in him merge with the man who loved the wider world. Introspection (and he wrote part of his first book actually sitting in front of a mirror) married to an infinite curiosity. It's a difficult balance to strike.

More controversially, the ageing Gide had no truck with the myth that, as you grow old and lose your sap, you should just smile serenely and rejoice in the spiritual profundity that allegedly takes root in your decaying flesh. Released at last from the mad stranglehold of carnal desires, according to this myth, you are free to peacefully ponder higher things while the young make whoopee. In Victor Hugo's famous and fatuous phrase, the flame in the eyes of the young turns in the old man's eyes into pure light. In fact, the milkiness is just as likely to be cataracts. Even in earlier, slower times when accumulated wisdom carried some weight, not everyone was seduced by the beatific humbug of old age drained of carnal desire. Montaigne, for instance, once said something pithy about refusing to thank impotence for the kindness it did him, while Schopenhauer lamented the 'mere shell' that remains once the sexual urge has been 'burnt out'. All the same, the idea of spiritual profundity redeeming the sexual numbness of old age still has a certain appeal in fast-moving, highly mobile societies like ours where the body is the only presence we have time to recognise and sexual attractiveness an eye-catching accessory. Look young, look fecund. If that's a tall order at your age, then ... what about 'spiritual profundity'? (Plus minding the grandchildren.) Since 'spiritual profundity' has no precise meaning, this phrase makes everyone feel a lot better. It offers comfortingly vague links to a slower world where people had time to recognise presences in more deeply rooted ways.

Yet lurking somewhere in that phrase—the fuzzy word 'spiritual' being the culprit, I suspect—is a delicate avoidance of saying outright what those in the prime of life really think happens when you grow old: you become an idiot, a witless old nark with nothing much of any use to say about life *now*. Nowadays, not only do the young Google anything they need to know, they occasionally even Google *us* as they hurry past, downloading some useful snippet of information they couldn't find elsewhere. For the most part, though, yesterday's wisdom is today's senile gobbledygook.

Worse than that, 'spiritual profundity' hides a distaste—even repugnance—for the alarming idea that the sagging and stiff-jointed are still sexual beings. Gide wasn't having any of it. He wanted to be *more* present in the world, not less, as he grew older. 'There was once a time,' he wrote in his diary at the age of seventy-two, 'when, tormented to the point of anguish and plagued by desire, I would pray: oh let the time come when my curbed flesh allows me to give my self over entirely to ... But to give myself over to what? Art? "Pure" thought? God? What ignorance! What madness! It was the same as believing that the flame would burn brighter in a lamp with no oil left in it. When it is abstract, my thinking is extinguished. Even today, it is the fleshly in me that feeds the flame, and today I pray that I might remain fleshly and full of desire until I die.' Like Camus' Clamence in *The Fall*, Gide found himself liking life in the world so much that he had no imagination when it came to any other kind.

His prayer seems to have been answered. Two years later, for instance, in the stifling heat of Gao, Mali, while waiting for repairs to be made to his aircraft, he enjoyed 'one of the most vivid' experiences of carnal delight of his life. All his memories of Gao are 'bathed in the radiance' of this encounter. 'I have not succeeded in despising carnal delights,' he noted in his diary, 'and in any case make hardly any effort to do so.' At the age of seventy-eight he remarked contentedly that he felt 'no shame at all after casually indulging in carnal pleasures'. It was, he confessed, to delight in 'a sort of vulgar paradise, a communion from below. The important thing is not to give it any importance, nor to believe that you've been abased by it: the mind is in no way involved in it, nor the soul, either, which hardly pays it any attention. But in an adventure such as this, the joy of discovery, of something new, is accompanied by an extraordinary sense of fun and pleasure.'

No, for Gide (infuriatingly, as far as the moralists were concerned) it wasn't a matter of choosing between 'the bliss of the flesh' and that deepening of the spirit that is supposed to characterise old age: he'd been deepening his spirit since childhood, and continued to accumulate wisdom, embellish his intellect, refine his feelings and abundantly feed what once would have been called his 'soul' until the day he lay unconscious on his deathbed (Virgil on the table beside him). He had a passion for endlessly renewing his acquaintance with the world. He simply rejoiced in whatever opportunities presented themselves to live out what he had imagined as a youth. While there was oil in his lamp, he was happy to let it burn.

There is no great mystery about why. 'They say I'm running after my youth,' he wrote in his diary at fifty-two. 'It's true. And not only after my own.' A few years later he was even more explicit: straightjacketed inside his mother's Calvinist religion until he fled to Tunisia, he missed out on 'the delights of the flesh' when he was an adolescent and spent the rest of his life 'repenting' with a fervour that many found indecent, to say the least. He knows that it's unseemly but he doesn't try to excuse his lifelong attempt to recapture an adolescence he never had. Which, he asks on the cusp of sixty, is worse?

> To shun pleasure when you are young or to look for it when old? There is a kind of bliss of the flesh that the ageing body pursues more and more pointlessly, unless it has indulged itself to excess when young. An overly chaste youth leads to a dissolute old age. It is doubtless easier to give up what you've known than what you imagine. It is not what one has done that one misses now, but what one hasn't done or could have done.

Gide regretted his youthful chastity until the day he died. He knew perfectly well that in the autumn of life (a cliché he used himself) one's pleasure at being alive would necessarily have a different colouring from the one it had at sixteen or thirty. Apart from anything else, the flesh is less turbulent, however active the libido, which is just as well because opportunities for pleasure become fewer, at least in the Western world. But he saw no reason to wash all the vibrancy of youthful sexuality out of old age and colour it 'soulful' instead. 'It is no more fitting to see in old age nothing but a decline,' he wrote at the age of fifty-nine, 'than it is to regard youth as nothing but promise. Each age is capable of its own particular kind of perfection. It is an art to convince yourself of this, to focus on what the years bring us, rather than on what they deprive us of, and to prefer gratitude to regret.'

In Western societies, as we know, the very suspicion that an ageing male might be living out his sexual fantasies arouses either ridicule or disgust. While a lustful young man is exciting, romantic, charming, disarming and dangerous in a delectable way, a lustful old man is disturbing, repellent, ludicrous and dangerous in a frightening way, unless it's some Greek god (Zeus abducting his cup-bearer Ganymede, for instance, and even that is best not thought about in too much detail these days). While the idea of lustful elderly women is almost too outlandish to entertain—the very phrase sits oddly, it smacks of bawdy comedy tinged with the grotesque—for lustful old men we have a vocabulary of disgust: they're 'dirty old men' (*vieux cochons* in French—'old pigs'), 'lechers' and 'old pervs' (a 'pervert' rarely being younger than the object of his desire and never more attractive). They 'make a nuisance of themselves', 'bothering' the young and attractive or 'preying' on them shamelessly. It's true that older men of a certain class (barristers, prominent businessmen or sporting heroes) might get away with being scalliwags, but only so long as they restrict themselves to the occasional good-humoured outburst of outrageous behaviour that everyone can have a good laugh at—pinching a waitress's bottom, for instance, or turning their amorous adventures into a bit of bar-room bragging. Somewhere around the onset of middle age any man with a sense of his own dignity is supposed to douse his libido and don a mantle of serenity, fondling his wife occasionally, perhaps, but in the main devoting himself to pruning the roses, developing an interest in something (home improvements, collecting model cars—anything), dining out with friends from time to time and managing his infirmities until such time as they get the better of him. Gide did all these things, as it happens, apart from the model cars, but much else besides, becoming more and more inquisitive about the world as he grew older, rather than less. He did not sink into sexless serenity.

As any older person is, Gide was, however, acutely aware of what he called the 'aesthetic' problem. I was myself, as I handed Giovanni his silver tray and he stretched out his firm, brown hand to take it. 'Old hands seem to wither what they caress,' Gide wrote, thinking no doubt of something more intimate than handing a tray to a waiter. It was this awareness, more than any moral consideration, he said, that prompted him to forgo the bliss he still ardently desired. When joined in prayer, he notes, old hands are allowed a certain beauty, but 'young hands are made for love's caresses, for garnishing love. It's a great pity to make them join in prayer too soon.' I somehow doubt that Giovanni's will be too hastily clasped in prayer—just a feeling I have.

In a city like Naples I am conscious every hour of the day of what an affront to youthful beauty the ageing body can be. I see it in the blank looks of young shop assistants and passers-by, in the quickly averted eyes as I pass the young in parks or enter a café. Keep your distance, they seem to be warning me, stay to one side, get out of my way, you've had your day. There's kindliness as well sometimes, that goes without saying, particularly in bookshops or museums, where maturity may have some value, but there, as in church, the aesthetics are different, as they are in family groupings. On the whole, though, I think Gide was right: there's something aesthetically troubling to us about ageing skin drawing close to the taut beauty of the young body. It's dispiriting to suspect that you've become repulsive to the young. It's not something I feel so keenly in North Africa, at least in those parts beyond the reach of modernity. Perhaps I wilfully misread those wantoning African eyes.

North Africa feels so close here in Naples, much closer than Milan or Florence do. It's tempting to believe that if I had a telescope I could see the smudge of Africa low on the horizon. Roman ships must once have set out across the bay below me for Carthage and Hippo, reappearing a few days later laden with corn, wine and olive oil. And in Africa I feel close to Rome. Just a couple of months ago, when I was back in Tunisia, with Daniel this time, we were jolting through the desert one morning in a jeep, weaving around dunes, ploughing through sand drifts and staring into a yellowish grey emptiness, when all at once we caught sight of a strange stone citadel on top of a sand hill far away to the east. It turned out to be a Roman frontier post, so well preserved after two thousand years that I wouldn't have been in the least surprised if a detachment of soldiers had come back from patrol and started roasting a gazelle for lunch right in front of us. But there was nobody there at all, apart from one old man wrapped in innumerable layers of rags against the cold wind, wanting to recharge his mobile phone in the jeep. (Which he did. It beeped: he had two messages.)

The desert has kept Rome alive in Africa, it has kept it imaginable in a way it rarely is in Italy. Even in Pompeii and Herculaneum, just around the bay from where I'm sitting, unless you go very early in the morning before the crowds start swarming all over them, it's hard to imagine yourself back in a living city, difficult to capture that sense of interrupted lives, even with Vesuvius still looming over you a few miles away to the east. In the winter of 1817, when tourists were presumably few, Stendhal went to Pompeii at least three times a week: 'it is the most astounding, the most interesting, the most amusing thing I have encountered', he wrote. 'It is only by going there that you can know antiquity ... you feel transported back to antiquity.' But I think he was mostly bowled over by the frescoes. Two hundred years later, to fill the streets and shops and villas with living people—sailors, slaves, surgeons, housewives, priests, painters, bakers, prostitutes, merchants, madmen, children running home from school—is almost impossible. It's hard to make your eyes see what they saw through the blur of Germans and Japanese. At that fort on the edge of the Sahara I saw exactly what the Romans had seen: sand and shadows, and the smudge of an oasis on the southern horizon at Ksar Ghilane.

With Daniel, I must say, although I must be older

than his father, I do not feel that aesthetic embarrassment that pinches at me whenever I draw close to someone young. For that matter, Albert is old enough to be his grandfather, yet I sensed no aesthetic clash watching them together, either. Perhaps they were two hands joined in prayer, though. For some reason Daniel's beauty is not a reproach. He's such a chameleon—I think that's why.

The impulse to draw closer to him, the muffled craving I feel when I'm with him for greater intimacy, is now probably about presences rather than merely bodies. Time has that effect. I hope that doesn't sound too 'spiritual'. What I want is to take *being with him* to a pitch. I said some of these things to him that night at Ksar Ghilane. I probably shouldn't have, but we were together in our tent under the palm trees on the fringe of the oasis. I'd just watched him swimming alone in the hot spring in the velvety darkness. Close by there'd been Tuaregs softly drumming on their goatskin drums. The moment had seemed right.

I imagine that his lips were beginning to curl in one of his sardonic smiles, but it was too dark to see. All he said was: 'What are you worried about? To me you just look like you. Listen, I'm whacked. Good night, sleep well!' He's never very wordy.

How could I explain to the young man I'd watched slicing so effortlessly through the water an hour before in the hot spring, bending like a dancer from the waist to dry his toes, hurtling through the trees in the cold moonlight to the tent like a startled deer, that I could have done the same thing if it hadn't been for the ridiculous scarecrow's costume somebody had laced me up in. That's how it feels. This is not me, I wanted to say, I've just been done up to look like this.

Albert is marvellous on this subject. A few years ago, while visiting him in his bookshop in Montpellier, I told him how shocked I'd been the day before when I'd run into a friend from my university days, someone I hadn't seen for over forty years. I'd been buying an ice-cream at one of those kiosks in the old quarter when the woman waiting next to me turned to me and said: 'Robert! Fancy running into you again after all these years—and in Montpellier of all places!' I looked at her carefully: nothing. A grandmotherly-looking woman, stoutish, hair dyed auburn, a few wrinkles about the eyes and mouth, lipstick a shade too bright ... surely nobody I knew. 'Andrea,' she said. 'Don't you remember? Sydney University, 1961.' I remembered Sydney University in 1961 (vaguely), but not this woman, whatever her name was. She looked slightly nonplussed, but kept smiling. 'Molière. *Le Malade imaginaire.* I was Angélique, and you were my lover.' I was appalled. 'Cléante, wasn't it? "*Je vous aime, je vous aime.*" You can't have forgotten.' Was this woman with thick ankles and a slight pot, to be frank, completely mad? And then it came back to me with a jolt. Of course—Andrea. A dark-eyed wisp of a girl, she'd worn mulberry lipstick when no one else had dared to, and at the party after the show she'd danced the tango with *her brother*, it had been electrifying, he was like a rapier ... it all came flooding back. 'Andrea! Good grief! What are you doing in Montpellier?' As if it mattered. But I had to say something while the image in my mind struggled to superimpose itself on the woman my eyes were resting on. Then with a click it succeeded. I have no idea how. There was no connection between the two. By focusing on the eyes, I suppose. And the voice. The disguise she was wearing just fell away.

'Ah, yes, disguise,' Albert said with a chuckle, reaching under his desk for a well-thumbed volume. It was Proust, as it turned out, and I remember him reading out some delicious passages describing the narrator entering a crowded room at the Guermantes' to find acquaintances from long ago so changed that he had the impression that they were in fancy dress. There was the suave diplomat who was playing the part of an old dodderer, and an old enemy, M. d'Agencourt, who was dangling like 'a quivering puppet with a false beard of white wool ... being put through its paces'. It was a theatrical pageant, a pantomime, an animated collection of masks or bad portraits. They were not old men, Proust wrote, 'they were young men of eighteen at an advanced stage of withering'. To turn one 'lithe fair-haired girl', a marvellous waltzer in her youth, into 'the corpulent white-haired lady making her way past me with heavy tread

... this potbellied old field marshal, it must have been necessary for life to accomplish a vaster work of demolition and reconstruction than is needed to replace a steeple with a dome ...' But what really struck me, I remember to this day, was the word 'attachment': at some point Proust says that one guest, M. de Cambremer, had been made unrecognisable by the *attachment* of huge red pouches to his cheeks so that he could scarcely open either his mouth or his eyes. Taking it to be some form of anthrax, the narrator waits for his friend to mention his unfortunate disfigurement, but, like some courageous invalid, he doesn't. That's precisely it: something has been tied onto us, hobbling us, making us look like clowns. I've never read much Proust, I never seem able to get past the first volume, he simply tells me more about everything and everybody than I want to know; but when Albert read those passages out in that smoky voice of his, eyes dancing, I remember thinking I really should give *Remembrance of Things Past* another go.

And what do these Punch and Judy caricatures see when they first clap eyes on us? That's another unsettling question. Was Andrea aghast at my impersonation of a skeleton? If so, she didn't show it. She just chatted on from inside her fat lady's costume about her children and grandchildren, as people do when they haven't seen you for a long time, presuming for reasons I can't begin to imagine that you'd be interested. Then we wandered off in different directions, rather like the guests at the Guermantes' party, hardly caring, despite the warmth of our goodbyes, whether or not our paths ever crossed again.

'Ah yes, parties,' Albert murmured, putting the Proust to one side. '*Les fêtes*. I almost never go to them nowadays—a few drinks after a book launch sometimes here in the shop, that's about all I can be bothered with at my age.'

'But you like people . . . you still see the folk from the walking group, don't you? And you've got people coming into the bookshop all day.'

'Oh, yes, I like people, I'm not cut out to be a hermit.'

'Then what is it about parties?'

He thought about it for a moment, his eyes resting on the street outside. An old woman sat in a window opposite, staring back down. 'I think I've finally lost interest in rituals of renewal, and that's what parties are at root, I'm sure of it.'

'You mean Christmas and birthdays and so on?'

'I mean almost any sort of party, really.'

'But what's wrong with renewing old friendships, for example?'

'Nothing, I suppose.'

'And don't we go to parties to open up new possibilities sometimes, to meet new people, to . . .'

'Feel young again?' 'No, not just that.'

'I haven't closed myself off to new possibilities, I love sitting at the cross-roads, so to speak, you know I do, waiting to see who might come by. Every time the door opens here in the shop and that little bell jingles I come alive. No, it's something else I'm tired of.'

'What?'

In his birdlike way he studied the old woman in the window across the road who seemed to be studying us. 'She's there every afternoon, that woman. Never reads, never even knits, just sits and looks. I keep expecting her to stand up one day and throw herself out. I would if I were her. But what is it I'm tired of? Rituals, I think. You'll think I'm an old curmudgeon, but when I first arrive at a party, when I enter the room, I feel my heart sink. Sometimes I enjoy chatting with someone new for a while, or seeing someone again after some months or years, but I can't be bothered any more with the ceremony of making myself acceptable, desirable (and I mean that in the haziest way possible) yet it seems to me that people traipse off to parties as much as anything to renew their desirability—as friends, as companions, as people worth knowing. They dress for it, they trot out all their best lines, put on a little act, ingratiate themselves one way or another. There's a ritualised coquetry about parties, don't you find? Now, what I like to do is to find a quiet spot somewhere, especially outside if it's warm enough, and sit there with an old friend, someone I don't have to renew anything with, and just deepen what we've got.'

'But isn't that a kind of renewal of something? Aren't

you polishing up a friendship?'

'But it's not a ritual. It's the thing itself—this *is* our friendship, like this moment with you. When I look at my watch and see it's time to think about leaving, what I want to do most of all is savour the continuity, the feeling that some things in life are richer than I remembered and are going to last. It's about sustaining something, not renewal. As for the grand rituals of renewal—New Year's Eve, those orchestrated mass rituals at football matches, anniversaries of every description, and especially Christmas, that renewal of hope in something I don't hope for, not wanting to be 'saved'—well, I lost interest in all that decades ago. I'm still curious, but I don't hope. I find it's better that way. You'll understand one day, I'm sure.' (I know why he says that, but wish he wouldn't.)

I fingered a vegan cookbook while I thought about this. Five-spiced tofu in soy sauce—now *that* would be worth waiting all day for. 'What about your own religious rituals? What about your yoga, for instance?'

'Yoga isn't a ritual. Yoga is being. And I don't worship, haven't you noticed? I have no altar. Why worship? Who exactly do worshippers think needs their adoration or needs to be placated? It's infantile. I seek to understand.' I wondered fleetingly about the candlelit image of his Living Goddess, but said nothing. One more syllable and we'd tip over into the 'spiritual'. However tempting it was to coax him to say more, I didn't want to end up listening to a lecture on the Five Forms of Vishnu, which is the direction we were slewing in.

I have nothing against 'religion'—that neverending, many-sided conversation about transcending the observable universe—but Albert, it seems to me, has mistaken a colourful myth for a report on the way things are. Religion, to give it its due, is part of the world, and I'm curious about the world, although whether my curiosity has retained the *'allégresse presque fringante'* (almost frisky cheerfulness) that Gide said characterised his at eighty, I'm not so sure. It may all be humbug, a science without a discernible subject (as one disillusioned vicar described it to me), but I like to listen in to the discussion from time to time just in case it isn't. The trick would be to transcend time and space while loving what we find there. As a rule all I can hear, though, is people either revelling in their own emotions or ventriloquising some exalted version of themselves. However, when I do listen, I do so with one eye on my own spiritual plumb-line, mysteriously ordering the arabesques of words and deeds in my everyday life, and this plumb-line has nothing to do with Vishnu. Or the Holy Trinity or Allah. To be candid, it now never will.

For Sartre, God ceased to exist without a word of warning: one day while waiting for his schoolmates he decided to think about God and, to his 'polite surprise', God just 'tumbled into the blue and disappeared without giving any explanation'. And that was that.

For others of us His departure is less abrupt. Although André Gide, for instance, was already playing cat and mouse with God before he left for Tunisia the first time, and although his religious imagination eventually failed him and he decided it had all been a mirage, for most of his life he kept asking God to account for His failure to appear.

In the mid-1930s, with spectacularly bad timing, he even seems to have hoped that the Kingdom of God might have come to earth in the form of the Soviet Union. While visiting Moscow as a hugely fêted guest of the Writers' Union, he even allowed himself to appear in Red Square in the company of Stalin, Molotov and other psychopathic mass-murderers, babbling on about how the fate of culture depended on the USSR which he would passionately defend—at least as long as he was a hugely fêted guest of the Writers' Union. To give him his due, once he got back to France, he told the truth about this land of lies and brutally enforced conformity to Marxist dogma. It's a wonder that the Soviet officials hadn't foreseen this: as Aleksandr Arosev, the Chair of the All-Union Society of Cultural Relations with Foreign Countries, warned before he arrived, 'Gide's peculiarity is that he is a man of extremely shaky principles'. For this reason, he instructed, every effort was to be made to 'maintain the illusion of spontaneity' during his visit because, if there's one thing men of shaky principles jib at, it's any hint of a prearranged schedule. Gide was not fooled and Arosev was later shot. Ideology of any kind seems to have lost its gloss for Gide after that failed experiment.

Anyway, no sooner had Albert said 'I seek to understand' than the bell above the door jingled and two schoolgirls came in, smirking with that peculiar mixture of sauciness and bashfulness that schoolgirls cultivate. I slipped out into the street and left Albert sitting sharp-eyed at his crossroads.

In bed that night in Ksar Ghilane, after Daniel had curled up to sleep, my mind kept fiddling with that conversation in the bookshop, trying to piece it together again to give me strength. Daniel loved parties, I remembered. He also hopes. His life has a completely different rhythm from mine, or Albert's. But that's also one of the things I like about travelling with him.

Perhaps it's even the main thing. Gide always travelled with younger companions, not, as the pursed-lipped moralists would have it, in order to take advantage of them sexually (sex was too light a pleasure, as far as he was concerned, to weigh it down with all the formalities that that would have required), but to stop one thing seeming to him as good as another, which can happen as you grow older: Charles Trenet, Joan Sutherland, a rainbow, your new Toyota, dinner at Le Grand Véfour, a takeaway cheese sandwich in the Place de la République ... it can all start to sound and look and taste much the same. 'The last act flags,' as he put it, musing on 'the end of life'. 'Reminders of the past, the pointless repetition of things already said. One would like some unexpected development to occur and does not know what to come up with.' It's not just a matter of the last act flagging, though: the worst part is that you come to suspect that the whole play has been a mishmash of inconsequentialities from the first word of Act I. Spending time with the young, and especially travelling with them, traversing the landscape in a series of improvised sorties, can lead to all sorts of unexpected developments, since nothing anchors them; but most valuably of all it reimmerses you in an earlier act in the play: there the plot is forever thickening promisingly, you watch life's drama through different eyes. The rhythm is different. At any rate, that's the theory.

Gide, with his tumultuous erudition, liked to think of himself as playing a Socratic role with the young as well: his letters, and no doubt his conversation, were full of advice on what to read, how to behave, where to go, how to think. He liked to imagine that the old should resign themselves to giving to the young, expecting little in return. Perhaps the young in his day were more accustomed to sitting at the feet of the old and learning, but I don't find them much inclined to do that these days. Daniel, for instance, darts in and out of my store of experience on a whim. 'Do you feel really passionate about anything?' 'Why do you like Bonnard?' 'What was it like in Moscow in the sixties?'—he wants to learn, but loathes being taught. I can sometimes feel him about to swoop like a kingfisher into my stream, but once he's caught his fish he soars away from me again and I lose sight of him. It's exhilarating, but not Socratic.

When I woke up next morning shivering under my blankets to an orchestra of bird calls, he had already disappeared (along with everyone else, it seemed). The whole camp, I discovered, was out on the dunes watching the sun rise. Daniel was no doubt one of the dozens of black dots far out amongst the frozen ripples of sand, which were turning pink, then golden, then amber and tawny-yellow before my eyes. For one eerie moment I was tempted to drop to my knees and chant my adoration of the molten disk floating on the horizon. In the cold, boundless stillness of that moment nothing yet existed but the sun. I'd shrunk to nothing. And then, teetering on the verge of ecstasy, I thought of breakfast.

Once the sun had climbed well up into the sky, people started to trickle back to the oasis for their coffee and baguettes, Daniel amongst them, radiant in his red anorak and scarlet beanie. After squinting at the snaps he'd just taken out on the dunes on his digital camera (sun, sky, sand, as you'd expect) I scrolled through the dozens of shots he'd taken in Tunisia while he savoured the quince jam and his own elation. This is another reason for spending time with the young, we're told: it's refreshing to see the world through their eyes. His eyes had focused on dark alleyways ending in a burst of blinding light; peeling, pitted walls glowing in a shaft of sunlight; a canary in a cage at an open window; a wrought-iron arabesque, sky-blue, encasing an empty window; a door, tomato-red, in a lettuce-green wall; a chequerboard of roof gardens; the shadow of a minaret across a square; a tiled courtyard awash with light ... his mornings in the medinas (Tozeur, Douz, Sfax, Mahdia) had been utterly different from mine. He'd wandered them (by my side) like a young Matisse in the making, collaging brilliant patterns of colour and shade. I'd always been Gide, noting faces, ready to dally with anyone loitering with a smile on a street corner, reading inscriptions, pondering the history of the Great Mosque. Daniel hadn't even bothered photographing the Great Mosque. He would wait while I bantered with fruit sellers and boys sitting idly in the sun, gazing up at window frames in teetering walls, peering inside half-open doorways to sniff at the dank air inside, disappearing into mud-brick tunnels, angling for a shot of white-on-white-on-white—sheets on a wall backed by clouds. Momentary bursts of light. It was refreshing seeing these towns through his eyes, but hardly illuminating. He didn't know enough about what he was looking at to make it illuminating. It was like Stendhal's Lethe, come to think of it. Being with Daniel is drinking the waters of Lethe, but the forgetfulness never lasts.

He left me suddenly without even finishing his coffee to try to find again a Tuareg scarf stall he'd passed at dawn. Daniel's head wrapped in one of those violent blue Tuareg scarves would be more than merely eye-catching. I scrolled through a few more captured moments, then sauntered outside and headed off down the first path I saw into the palm grove, trying to see it as Daniel might have, stripped of words. I couldn't. I'm really hopeless at oblivion, however hard I try. Language doesn't matter to him in the way it does to me. For me nothing has the substance of words any more. There's music, it's true, but not even Beethoven or Bach transport me utterly. I wish it weren't true, but I wonder sometimes if I could even love if I couldn't find the right words for it. I think of Gide lamenting the fact that language takes up so much of his time in old age: 'Worrying about how to say things—it's a bad sign,' he said (at the age of fifty-nine). 'It's my constant preoccupation during the short time I have left to live; you couldn't find a sillier way to spend it. It's like someone continually consulting his watch for fear of missing his train. "Don't get yourself into such a state. It won't leave without you."'

Needless to say, there's a danger in wanting to live through someone younger—well, through anyone at all, really. You can begin by wanting to see the world through their eyes and end up forgetting who you are. Or worse. As Gide wrote to Marc Allégret from Algiers some twelve years after falling in love with him: 'Fearing that I was living too much through you, I wanted to leave you for a time. I am no longer living at all. I'm getting ready to come back. But will I find you in Paris?'

Marc, however, was Gide's *beloved*. (Whatever Daniel was to me—my young self, for instance, alert to the merest flicker of desire—he wasn't my beloved.)

Gide wasn't infatuated with Marc by the time he wrote that letter, nor pining like a troubadour at his castle gates. Marc wasn't even the object of his desire any more: he was his beloved. It was all very Turkish—sixteenth-century Turkish, to be precise. It was also very Japanese: in Japan relations between an older man and a younger beloved (monk and acolyte, samurai warrior and adolescent samurai, theatre patrons and kabuki actors) flourished over centuries. There are love poems by Buddhist priests addressed to their beloved acolytes dating from the tenth century. This sort of love, reviled to the point of hysteria in our society, was part of classical court culture in Japan. Yet it's Turkey, not Japan, that comes to mind when I think of Gide and Marc. There was something too theatrical, too rehearsed, too bound up with Buddhist thought about the custom as it was played out in Japan for me to picture a strong link to Gide. In the Japanese tradition the beloved youth was likely to turn out to be the incarnation of a Bodhisattva, thereby saving the monk's soul. This wasn't Gide's style at all. In Turkey the connection between loving these tulip-cheeked flirts with necks like camphor candles and loving God was much more blurred. Gide didn't take to Constantinople when he eventually went there in 1914, finding the people 'universally ugly', but if he'd found himself there four hundred years earlier it might have been a very different story.

If a wizard had cast a spell on Gide and sent him hurtling back four centuries to the Constantinople of Süleyman the Magnificent, he'd have undoubtedly thought that he'd woken up in paradise. If he'd dropped in for a cup of wine to any of the taverns in the centre of the city or mixed with other guests at a garden party beside the Bosphorus, he'd have noted with delight that, while men married, loved their wives and regarded any display of effeminacy with contempt, they at the same time openly cultivated another kind of love, one he'd caught the mere echo of in the casbah in Algiers (which, when it was first built, housed the janissaries of none other than Süleyman the Magnificent): love for a beloved.

Given his enthusiasm for classical poetry, Gide would obviously have first recalled the racy, iconic story of Zeus abducting Ganymede and making him his wine-pourer. In any tavern he found himself in he'd have become aware before too long of a playful, erotic connection between some of these young heart-thieves, with their moon-shaped faces and delicate waists, and some of their older customers. And he'd have understood exactly what he was looking at.

Somewhat later in the century, in the coffee houses that began appearing in the city in 1552, he'd have noticed a subtle change in the games being played. Here he'd have been surrounded by a more educated clientele, still engaged in noisy conversation, as in the taverns, but also reading poetry aloud to each other, quite often their own, playing board games, listening to music, telling stories, watching boys and girls dancing, enjoying a performance of shadow puppets. There'd have been the odd bootmaker, tailor and silk merchant's son amongst the crowd, no doubt, but also muezzins, magistrates and teachers. He couldn't have missed the small heart-softening gestures and looks that passed between some of the bearded patrons and their beardless companions, and, with the gift of tongues, he'd have been astonished by the cascade of epithets for the young beloveds in every dizzying *ghazel* he heard read out—supple as a cypress, jasmine-breasted, hair sweeter-smelling than ambergris and so on. Again, I think he'd have understood what he was looking at in a way that most of us would not. He'd seen something similar in the *karagouz* (shadow-puppet) theatres of Tunis.

Had he been invited to a garden-party in one of the more aristocratic districts, where men gathered with their beloveds, or in particular into one of the kiosks in his host's garden, he could well have found a much more overt display of courtship rituals—and, possibly, in behind the lilac bushes amongst the trailing jasmine, of their rapturous conclusion as well. In the progression from tavern to private party and secluded kiosk, Gide would have observed a kind of refinement of the play that Turks indulged in—the explicit lines of poetry, the reciprocal glances, the gestures of intimacy, the flirtatiousness of the beloveds, the simmering rivalry between their swains.

What Gide would have seen in the houses and squares of Constantinople was a ritual of exchange between 'lover' and 'beloved'. As in Tunis today, or in Paris, for that matter, the bargain could be quite crude: a clog-maker's son or butcher's lad had little to offer an admirer except his body and the admirer little to offer in exchange except money or a gift. For that matter, Ganymede had nothing to offer Zeus except his body and a bit of table service, although in his case the reward was immortality—not a bad deal, he was obviously a heart-snatcher of the first order. And the streets of Turkish cities also teemed with young toughs and soldiers on leave whose idea of an exchange was often not just crude but violent, exactly as in Tunis or Paris today. None of this would have surprised Gide. What was different about sixteenth-century Turkey was the possibility for another kind of barter which in modern Christian societies has been squeezed out of existence between two erotic monoliths: prostitution on the one hand and marriage on the other. For us, in other words, there is just the brothel (in some form or other) and the home. In the space between them there is nothing much left these days except a bit of harmless sport and shopping.

Before the puritans took over, the Turkish lands offered educated males another, more nuanced option: the exchange between an older 'lover' and a younger 'beloved'. In return for what we might broadly call 'patronage'—invitations, introductions, wisdom, uplifting company—the younger man, still downy-cheeked, not bearded (because two bearded men with any self-respect could only contemplate a relationship between two equals) would offer at the very least his shy beauty, his affection and his poetry. At the very least there was an exchange of 'spiritual gifts': the older man 'hunted gazelles with *ghazels*', as they said, and the younger man sang him love songs back. Affection may or may not have shaded into something more carnal: from a Turkish point of view at the time, although not every imam's, love had many shades, and, so long as it was understood as basically a yearning for oneness with the Divine Bridegroom, it could be accommodated. There were ways. In our Christian society love of whatever hue, especially for men, is locked up at home. Escape is treacherous.

It's in this sense that I see Marc Allégret as Gide's 'beloved', although when Gide wrote him that frank letter about living through him too intensely Marc was well beyond the downy-cheeked stage. By this time he was definitely *exoletus*, as the Romans termed it: 'past it'. For over thirty years there was an exchange of feelings, ideas, letters, even 'poetry' in the broadest sense; they travelled together, worked together on various projects; Gide adopted him as his 'nephew', which gave a family name to a relationship which began with Gide being Marc's 'uncle'. 'Families, I hate you', but families give us all the best names.

With Pompeii and Paestum just down the road, and both Constantinople and Marc Allégret on my mind, the roof garden at the Hôtel Britannique is a good place to decide what I think about pederasty. I saw a bit of it, as a matter of fact, at the National Archeological Museum here in Naples this morning. It's in the Gabinetto Segreto (the Secret Cabinet), which is open only at special times and requires a special entrance ticket—a sop to the Vatican, which objects to its being open to the public at all. As a result of these restrictions, once you gain admittance, the crowds inside are so immense that you can hardly see the erotica you came to enjoy. However, if you're patient, among the wall-paintings, statues and ceramics from ancient sites depicting lascivious acts—everything from Pan fornicating with a goat to the various services available at a brothel (foreign sailors, speaking no Latin, preferred to choose from an illustrated menu) and dozens of 'unsheathed swords', as my guidebook calls them—there are several pieces that unashamedly celebrate pederasty. There's Pan, for instance, impressively horned, bearded and furry-legged, fondling a naked youth playing a mouth organ; a man on a horse eyeing off an extremely well-endowed young grape-picker; and one or two more equivocal pieces where the age of the revellers is hard to determine. (Gide did visit this museum, but was bored, finding it *'poncé, poncif'*—not raw enough, unoriginal. But he visited it before the Gabinetto Segreto was opened.)

Amorous relations between older men and adolescents may not have raised many eyebrows in Greece, Rome or sixteenth-century Turkey—they were obviously less threatening to the family and the social order than relations with other men's daughters or wives—but they're a very delicate matter indeed today. In those societies it was relations between adult men which were frowned on: since the sexual act implied domination and submission, relations between equals provoked mockery and disgust. Samuel Pepys, for instance, in seventeenth-century London wondered, while contemplating 'the Italian sport of buggery', a 'sin' he claimed not to know the meaning of, 'which is the agent [and] which is the patient'. We don't view sexual roles quite so rigidly these days, so answer the question about whom it is appropriate to love rather differently.

I think it is appropriate to love whoever knowingly invites our love and—this is the modern bit—enjoys it. (By no means all the youths and maidens in the Gabinetto Segreto were either inviting amorous attention or enjoying it.)

Giovanni is serving the Dutch couple on the other

side of the roof garden their afternoon tea, bringing to mind a waiter at my hotel in Oporto, much older than Giovanni, well into his thirties, but with the same hyacinth curls and finely drawn crescent eyebrows. Moist of lip, as the Ottomans might have said, his glance a dagger. Now, this Ignácio unmistakably *invited* my love (let's call it), finding every excuse he could think of to linger at my table chatting, fiddling needlessly with the flower arrangement and asking me if I'd like to go out for a drink with him when he finished work. Towards midnight, however, when we met up outside the station, and I asked him point blank what he enjoyed doing—it's best to know what you're in for—he wouldn't answer. He wouldn't admit to *enjoying* anything. He now held no more erotic interest for me than the can of Coca-Cola in his hand (which I'd paid for). I was going to buy him a coffee in a cosy bar somewhere and then put him in a taxi to go home, but the Holy Spirit Bank (the Banco Espirito Santo), informed, perhaps, of my epiphany that morning in the cathedral, declared my card invalid, so, having no money, I left him at the station looking puzzled, trying to sort out, presumably, what had gone wrong.

We don't love in a vacuum, though, I know. It may be appropriate, from my point of view, to love whoever knowingly invites our love and enjoys it, but not just anywhere at any time, regardless of the law or the consequences. An important question to ask, aside from what the law is (and the law has to draw a line somewhere), is whether or not anyone will be hurt or damaged—loved ones and family in particular, as well, of course, as the lovers themselves. In our present society every care is taken to make sure that *somebody* will be damaged severely, unless the union has been officially blessed.

Unwanted physical intimacy can be nauseating, even with a spouse. I hold no brief at all for those predators who sniff around our schoolyards, their pockets stuffed with lollies and lewd shenanigans with young bodies on their minds. Nor would Gide have held any brief for them: his ideal (rarely lived up to) was a kind of sensual chastity. In fact, his views on sex were so austere, so 'Greek', that he would have recoiled with distaste from men like myself, dismissing me as a 'sodomite'. Men who not only love men, but have relationships with men, struck him as disgusting. There was nothing 'gay' about André Gide.

Unlike Gide, I don't think sex is either good or bad unless it is. I just think it's something most human beings love doing with a chosen partner (or two)—and from an early age, too: as anyone who has travelled in a bus with a crowd of schoolchildren knows, ignorance about what would give pleasure fades away well before puberty. Sex may be more symphonic when orchestrated with deep feeling and joy in the other's good, but that's no reflection on a nice, brisk scherzo or even a jaunty jingle. At a concert in Paris recently I heard four brilliant variations by Franz Waxman on 'Auld Lang Syne'. It wasn't Mozart or Prokofiev, but it was sheer delight.

The trouble with Gide's predilections, it seems to me, is that on the sexual level, apart from Marc Allégret, jaunty jingles was all he was left with, the symphonies in his life being his loves and friendships, innocent of any note of sexuality. It might be a painless way to live, but it lacks something vitally human. 'My desire,' he wrote in *So Be It* just before he died, 'made up in part of curiosity, is very rapidly exhausted, and even, most commonly, when the pleasure is unalloyed, I find relief the first time around. I do not feel the need of either resumptions or repetitions.' This may have saved him a lot of heartbreak—an undeniable advantage when your desire targets the young—but surely it's a shallow sort of satisfaction. Often vivid, but one that needs to be constantly renewed with fresh, momentary objects of desire.

It's a Neapolitan (strangely enough, since I am in Naples), the Epicurian writer Lucretius, who springs to mind when I read lines like these. Gide's father had a copy of Lucretius in his library in Paris and Gide quotes him in his *Cahiers d'André Walter* as well as in his dairies. 'What male energy Lucretius has,' he noted in February, 1944, 'what austere nobility in his impiety, in his unruffled thought.' He even claimed to feel 'closer' to Lucretius than to his beloved Virgil. What made him feel 'closer' to Lucretius, I suspect, was Book IV of *On the Nature of the Universe* where the young Roman philosopher advises his readers to 'thrust from you anything that might feed your passion' for a love-object; to flee 'the certainty of heartsickness and pain' by 'lancing the first wound with new incisions, salving it, while it is still fresh, with promiscuous attachments... Do not imagine that by avoiding romantic love you are missing out on the delights of sex. Instead, you are reaping the sort of profits that carry with them no penalty. Be assured that this pleasure is enjoyed in a purer form by the sane than by the lovesick.' It's such a Gidean touch: sex untainted by romantic love is saner, more natural, even paradoxically purer, than the love that makes our breast 'burn with the evil lust of having'. Epicureans have the reputation of being gluttons and wine-bibbers, avid for bodily pleasure wherever they could find it, but their attitude to pleasure was surprisingly restrained. Lucretius, like his master Epicurus, was strict about avoiding those pleasures which ran the risk of causing pain, and nothing causes more misery than that 'drop of Venus' honey that first drips into our heart': the cost of sucking on it is unquenchable greed, jealousy, betrayal, enslavement to another's whim, bitterness, grief and downright madness. 'Take care,' Lucretius writes, 'not to get enmeshed.' Gide took great care indeed.

Whether Madeleine was damaged by Gide's behaviour or not is difficult to judge. She was certainly damaged as an adolescent by her mother's behaviour, and hurt by her husband's sinfulness, as she saw it: she feared his punishment would be eternal damnation. And she was horribly wounded by his affair with Marc Allégret; being abandoned at home for another, as she was when her husband took Marc to England, would crush anybody. For him there were many kinds of love; for her there were very few. That was the problem. On her twentieth birthday, some years before they married, she seemed to foresee the difficulties that might flow from joining her life to André's:

> 'This ability [of yours] to reflect every colour is a little too . . . chameleon-like. I can't properly see what place your own tastes occupy in the middle of this perpetual and universal consent to everything. Perhaps you extend eclecticism to the point of not having any tastes at all. Your admiration is a great caravanserai where everyone enters and is received with the same smile. Mine is a small temple where only the elect can pass inside.'

'She wrote that at twenty?' Zaïda exclaimed when I quoted that letter at dinner in Paris a few weeks ago. 'Brilliant! A caravanserai. I think I am a caravanserai.' She was certainly looking rather Berber that evening in her red caftan and her silver necklace embellished with turquoise gemstones.

'Nonsense,' Miriam said, 'you're just hopeless with men.'

'I like the idea of a caravanserai better.'

'Well, that makes me think of sweaty camel drivers and fleas.'

'You only say that because you're a small temple.'

We all gazed out of the window at the twilit streets of the 3rd arrondissement and thought about whether or not we were caravanserais or temples. Windows—hundreds of windows, row after row of windows, stretching away into the purplish gloom, some glowing, some dark. The street below us was empty. Even Yacoub, in whose honour this *dîner à quatre* had been arranged, stared out for a moment at the windows, although I don't imagine he felt compelled to choose between being a caravanserai or a temple.

Over the violet ice-cream, a startling concoction for which Zaïda had cadged the recipe from an Algerian friend of hers, Miriam and I finally agreed on one point: Madeleine Rondeaux and André Gide should never have married. But we arrived at our agreement from different directions. 'She could've made *him* happy, if he'd let her.'

'Happy!' I couldn't let that pass. 'She wanted him to be miserable—as miserable as she was. And in his misery turn to God and save his soul!'

Miriam ignored me. 'She could've made *him* happy, but he couldn't make *her* happy.'

'Not, as he said himself, without suppressing who he was. And what sort of happiness is that?'

'So he sacrificed her rather than himself.'

'Yes. "Warped her destiny" was the phrase he used. He had no illusions about what he'd done.'

'You Westerners,' Yacoub said with his usual elegant weariness, 'seem fixated on the idea of happiness. You chase after it everywhere, yet you never seem to catch hold of it. I understand pleasure, comfort, beauty, passion, peace, love ...'

'You? Love?' Zaïda was open-mouthed. A drop of violet ice-cream trickled down her chin.

'... but I don't understand what you mean by "happiness".'

'I can tell you,' I said, trying to head Zaïda off before she made a fool of herself. This was the woman who had once rung her lover to thank him for a bouquet of white roses he'd sent her for her birthday and *eaten* them, petal by petal, while they exchanged honeyed nothings across the Atlantic. 'Camus came up with the perfect definition.'

'Camus!' Zaïda looked puzzled. 'But he committed suicide, didn't he?'

'Not as far as I know. Anyway, what's that got to do with it? Clamence in *The Fall* says: "I took pleasure in my own nature, and we all know that that's what happiness is."'

'That's a rather self-satisfied, self-serving notion of happiness, don't you think?'

I didn't suppose that Miriam would give in without a tussle. 'What about ...'

'Feeding the hungry? Helping the blind to cross the street? I'm not talking about the morality of it, I'm just saying that that's what we Westerners, as Yacoub calls us, want in order to be happy: the right to take pleasure in our own nature as we see fit.'

'Whereas we Orientals only want the right to take pleasure in God's.' Yacoub smiled one of his smiles.

'But you don't believe in God—you told me so yourself in Blidah.'

'No, I don't believe in God, *and* I'm not an atheist.'

'That's not your line, that's Camus'!' Miriam loved finding chinks in her opponents' armour.

'What does it mean?' Zaïda asked. Nobody seemed to know, except possibly Yacoub, who wasn't saying, but I liked it. It summed up how I felt. She and Miriam went to the kitchen to prepare the coffee.

'So, did you find what you were looking for in North Africa?' Yacoub asked after a pause. I'd been waiting for him to ask. In the half-dark beside the window I could now barely make him out: just the glint of his cufflinks, the sheen on his silk tie, and the sharply etched line of one fine cheekbone.

'Well, it wasn't a quest, Yacoub.'

'You went there looking for *something*. What was it?'

'In the end you're asking me why I travel.'

'No, I'm asking you why you went to North Africa last year. It wasn't for the scenery.'

'No, it wasn't for the scenery. But to tell you why I went to North Africa, I'd have to start by telling you why I travel.' I considered the moon whose light Gide had thought so drinkable. 'When the absurdity of my life begins to nauseate me, I don't commit suicide, you see, I travel.'

'How could being in Algeria make your life less absurd? If life is nauseatingly absurd anywhere in this world, it's in Algeria.'

'It doesn't make *life* any less absurd, but for a few days, a week, a month, it can make mine seem worth living. I can take pleasure there in my own nature.' This sounded less flippant than Gide's observation about places where he found himself interesting—but it amounted to much the same thing, I suppose. 'In a way I can't at home—or at any rate not often.'

'Like Gide, do you mean? *Les petits musiciens*?'

'Yes and no, actually. Travel is an art, it seems to me, just like painting or writing a novel, it crystallises things. It crystallises me. Whenever I feel that I'm on the point of disappearing, dissolving into a thousand selves—and that happens when, like me and Gide, you don't feel you have a single source—I make art. I tell myself a story, I tell others a story, and I travel. And tell stories about my travels. I crystallise anew.'

'Did you crystallise at the St George in Algiers?'

'More in the casbah, I'd say.'

'Like Gide.'

'Thanks to Gide, rather than like him. There was no ecstatic moment with a young flute player. Young flute players really aren't my style.' Yacoub was almost invisible by now, but I'm quite sure he smiled. He knew precisely what I meant. However, before he could press me to say more, I seized the moment to resolve one small question about crystals. 'I make art—and travel—both to remember and to forget. Like a crystal, you see—both solid and translucent at the same time.'

'To remember and forget what, precisely?'

'To remember who I've been and also who I wanted to be, to write a new script and act it out without shame. To find my source.'

'That sounds like God again. And does it work?'

'No, of course not, but that's no reason to stay at home. But I also travel—and write—to forget, to sink into the river of unmindfulness, to be utterly transparent, crystal-clear, to just *be*.'

'And does that work?'

'For a day or two, if I'm lucky.'

'Biskra.'

'And the dunes around Ksar Ghilane. But I have to try. Remembering and forgetting, you see, that's what it's all about. Oases and deserts. North Africa is perfect.'

The smell of coffee drifted over us. Miriam and Zaïda appeared like two wraiths beside us in the darkness. Outside it had begun to drizzle. The roofs across the street were gleaming in the last tender wash of evening light. We had all disappeared.

♦

Last night here at the Hôtel Britannique, after dining downstairs alone with my memories, I had a dream I often have, although the details are different every time. I am at home, in my own house, this time a rambling blue and white mansion by the sea, empty and musty like a hotel out of season. Palm trees, cannas, cordylines, bursts of bougainvillea. I know it intimately, it's where I live, although I've also never seen it before in my life. I wander the creaking corridors, not exactly looking for anything, but expecting to find something. Here's a staircase I've never noticed before. I go up. I push open a door. And here I find a labyrinth of corridors and rooms I've never set foot in, never suspected existed. I'm astounded. It's full of life. Close friends and people I'd forgotten I knew (who seem now to be close friends) appear and disappear through doorways, gather around kitchen tables, play the piano, flirt, cavort and call to one another—even to me. My house is leading a double life.

At the end of the labyrinth I come to the strangest room of all: it's a tiny chapel, bathed in light. I know it's a chapel, although there's nothing religious about it at all: no altar, no pictures, no candles. It's bare. It only has three sides. The fourth wall is nothing but a curtain of thin gauze, ballooning gently in the breeze, letting the light from outside stream in. I can see the red blossoms on the trees outside in the garden, smell the sea. I sit down, the only member of the congregation. I am peacefully dead to myself.

    I wake up. I know why I'm here.

www.ingramcontent.com/pod-product-compliance
Lightning Source LLC
Chambersburg PA
CBHW031424150426
43191CB00006B/379